Absurd Tales from Africa

Robert Gurney

ISBN 978-0-9957601-6-5
Copyright ©2017 Robert Gurney
The right of Robert Gurney to be identified as the author of this work has been asserted by him in accordance with the Copyright, Designs and Patents Act, 1988
All rights reserved. No part of this publication may be reproduced, stored in retrieval system or transmitted in any form or by any means electronic, mechanical, photocopying, recording or otherwise, without the prior permission of the publisher, except in the case of brief quotations embodied in critical articles and reviews.
A CIP record for this book is available from the British Library
This work is a work of fiction. Names and characters are the product of the author's imagination and any resemblance to actual persons, living or dead, is entirely coincidental.

Published by
Llyfrau Cambria Books, Wales, United Kingdom.
Cambria Books is a division of
The Cambria Publishing Co-operative Ltd
Discover our other books at: www.cambriabooks.co.uk

Cover design by William Gurney

THE TALES

Author's Prologue	1
The Girl with the Glass Eye	4
The Dead Ringer of Rubaga	7
The Bell-Ringer of Montmartre	9
The Dust Devil Chaser of Amboseli	15
The Bowling Green Man of Entebbe	18
The Death's Head Hawk Moth Man of Makerere	22
The Englishman Called Hugh	26
The Fiendish Uganda Bookshop Plot	30
The Ghastly Soroti Coffin	33
The Giraffe Man Among the Twa	37
The Glutton of Namirembe	40
The Hills of Uganda	44
The Kampalan Clairvoyant	47
The Music Man of Kololo	50
The Lord of Nyamuliro	53
The Man with an Orange Head	58
The Missionaries of Bujumbura	61
The Naked Woman in the Kampala Odeon	64
The Nightmare on Makindye Hill	68
The Optometrist of Owino	71
The Original African Shaggy Dog Story	74
The Terrifyingly High Pier of Port Bell	77

The Sad Tale of Rwenzori Rory	84
The Talking Dog of Kisenyi	87
The Tin Man of Nakasero	90
Notes	95

Author's Prologue

The art of conversation, some say, is dying. Go into a restaurant and you will see couples sitting there silently texting. I asked one couple recently if they were texting each other. The lady blushed. Go into a pub and you will see people staring at TV screens. One where I live has at least six massive screens, two in the garden. Customers stare miserably at them. In other bars, loud music blares out, making conversation, other than a shouting match, impossible.

However, I do know of taverns where the "craic", the enjoyable conversation, still flows freely. The Shaggy Dog Story can form part of the fun. Stories can range from the obscene, to the sad and the totally absurd.

They nearly always end in a pun or punning phrase - there are many types - based on a distorted saying or catchphrase. They say the pun has been an essential part of English literature since *Beowulf* and before. Shakespeare was not averse to the odd one: "Now is the winter or our discontent / Made glorious summer by this sun of York." (*Richard III*, Act I, Scene I). "Puns are the highest form of literature." [!] (Alfred Hitchcock, TV interview with Dick Cavett, 1972.)

The stories in this book cultivate, in the main, the Absurd. One definition of the Absurd is that it is about the dysfunctional relationship between Man and his world. A sense of the Absurd comes from a feeling that things are just not working properly. The news was filled recently for days with stories about a singer song-writer I had never heard of.

The Spanish call shaggy dog stories "cuentos absurdos", absurd stories, the French, "histoires grotesques" or "histoires sans queue ni tête", stories without head nor tail. The English expression "I can't make head nor tail of it" must be related to the latter.

Literature of the Absurd has a strong presence in many cultures, especially those of English-speaking countries. Eugène Ionesco, Harold Pinter, Luis Buñuel, Camus (at school I was influenced by Camus' concept of absurdisme), Sartre, Stoppard and many others have exploited it. Children still read the "literary nonsense" novel *Alice's Adventures in Wonderland*, often shortened to *Alice in Wonderland* (1865), by the English mathematician Charles Lutwidge Dodgson, who used the pseudonym Lewis Carroll. My generation was brought up on the radio series The Goon Show. We were in that end-of-empire period in which old customs, habits, manners and ways of thinking were changing radically and were no longer appropriate. A friend of mine received one hundred pounds to buy a dinner suit before going out to Africa. He bought a pair of snake skin boots down the King's Road instead.

A shaggy dog story involves considerable build-up and convoluted action, resolved with an anti-climax or ironic reversal that renders the whole story meaningless. It may, perhaps, be the humblest example in the literary field but it is vigorous in oral, anglophone story-telling culture. It rests on the teller and the listener having a shared sense of the ridiculous. Life itself, after all, can often seem ridiculous. Instead of feeling tragic about it, as Unamuno, and at times, Dylan Thomas did, another possible reaction is to laugh at its absurdities.

On reading this book, the reader will say to himself or herself "I have heard that before". In many cases this will be absolutely true. The tradition of shaggy dog story-telling relies on a stock of familiar, formulaic and well-worn situations, retold in different contexts. Their number is limited by the small amount of surprising and acceptable puns available. The author makes no apology for going down this well-trodden path.

My father worked in a displaced persons' camps near Lecce in Italy during the Second World War. He used to tell this story.

A man would stand up and say "Numero quarantaquattro" (joke number forty-four). His colleagues fell about laughing. "Numero nove, number nine", he would shout. His companions beat the floor with their fists, roaring with laughter. "It's not what you say, it's the way that you say it that counts," he told me by way of explanation.

Acknowledgements

I would like to express my immense gratitude once again to Dr Clive Mann for his painstaking proof-reading of these stories. He did far more than that. He corrected factual inaccuracies and suggested ways in which the humour could be improved.

I would also like to thank, for their inspiration and suggestions, the small army of old Africa hands, fellow aid workers from the sixties and seventies, who have kept in touch with each other on both sides of the Pond and the Wall and who hold the occasional reunion, either here in London or in the USA.

Finally, I would like to thank my son William Gurney for providing the cover for this book.

The Girl with the Glass Eye

He was a shy sort of fellow, not very popular with his peers. He found himself one day waiting to meet a budding entrepreneur with a view to acting as a guide on trips to a little-known game area to the west of Kampala, Lake Mburu. He was going to report on his progress in securing basic accommodation there.

He was a little nervous, because he was not sure that he was allowed, as a civil servant, to engage in business activity. As he was still a DipEd student at Makerere, he had been trying to convince himself that a student could not be a civil servant at the same time. He still had a gap before that status kicked in, he said to himself.

His contact, a friendly chap who had approached him on one of his few visits to The City Bar restaurant - he wouldn't go into the bar - was late. Mark began to think that Philip was not going to turn up.

His mind began to turn to his special relationship with Dr Hughe Lee Dimwitty. He fed the latter with juicy titbits about fellow students' peccadilloes. It was he who had bought up some of Jones's lucky charms: bracelets that Jones claimed were made from his facial hair, although the rumour was that they were taken from an old Makerere mattress. Jones had been selling these to African tourists in the Speke Hotel, claiming they were "Mzungu Hair". Jones was at the top of Dr Carse's growing blacklist. The bracelets had been produced in front of the Professor of Education, Dr Lew Carse, during the trial *in absentia* after which Jones was ejected from East Africa.

They had chosen the Lake Victoria Hotel as the venue. TEA students, Teachers for East Africa, tended not to go there. It was too far from Kampala for them. He was contemplating his Pepsi, watching the remnants of the ice dissolve, when, suddenly, a huge sneeze interrupted his thoughts.

He looked up and his vision was filled with the sight of a beautiful young woman sitting by herself at the bar. It all happened in a flash. As his eyes focussed on her he saw an object flying towards him. He was a good cricketer and lunged forward to catch it. It was a glass eye!

Instinctively he leant forward and handed it back to her. She popped it back in.

"Come and talk to me," she said.

A wave of self-consciousness swept over him. He looked down at his shorts and became aware of his sartorial inadequacy. His shorts, he realised, were absurd. He hadn't thought about it before. They were brilliant white, like those of the other teachers at Makerere College School but they had shrunk through constant washing by the school's over-zealous laundryman. The result was that they were too tight, too short and tended to balloon out. From a distance it looked as if the staff were wearing nappies.

He dismissed these thoughts as he climbed up on to the bar stool.

She introduced herself as Margaret. She was, she explained, a secretary in Prime Minister Obote's Office at Entebbe and lived with two other secretaries in a large colonial bungalow in the bush off the Kampala to Entebbe Road.

He stared helplessly into her eyes and knew that he was in love, despite that fact that one of those eyes was false.

"Would you like to come back to my place?" she asked. He nodded, choking back a desire to confess that he was a twenty-three year-old virgin.

The following morning, Mark went down to the kitchen where Margaret was already busy.

"English breakfast?" she asked.

He nodded. He was lost for words. His whole world had suddenly changed. He felt as if it had been turned upside down.

Tongue-tied, he blurted out the following, without really thinking:

"Do you always do this with men you have just met?"

She gave him a quick look over her shoulder, her blue eyes sparkling.

"ONLY IF THEY CATCH MY EYE," she called out above the noise of sizzling sausages.

The Dead Ringer of Rubaga

The bell ringer at St Mary's Cathedral, Rubaga, in Kampala, retired after decades of service, so the priest placed an advertisement in the *Uganda Argus* for a new campanologist.

Kabaka Mutesa I Mukaabya Walugembe, the thirtieth Kabaka of Buganda, who reigned from 1856 until 1884, once maintained a palace where Rubaga now stands. He had abandoned the hill after the palace burned down following a lightning strike, giving the land to French missionaries, the White Fathers or "Wafaransa", as the locals called them. The Anglicans were put on Namirembe Hill, at a good distance from the Catholics, so that they could not engage easily and publicly in fisticuffs.

Anyway, the next day, Claude Pearman, a Bedfordshire man and a Philosophy and Religious Studies lecturer at Makerere University, arrived to apply for the vacancy. The advert had said, "No paperwork. Just turn up". The priest couldn't help noticing that his arms were in plaster and that each arm was supported by its own sling.

"What's wrong with your arms?" he asked Claude.

"I broke both of them during a rugby match between Makerere and Jinja. I tried to tackle a huge soldier from the barracks. Said his name was Amin."

Claude was a keen rugby player as well as an enthusiastic bell-ringer and an excellent philosopher to boot.

He didn't tell the priest but he had severe doubts about some aspects of Christianity but he loved the sound of bells, the camaraderie and the sheer physical exercise of pulling on the ropes. He comforted himself, when doubts assailed him, by rehearsing the steps of Pascal's 'Wager' on which he had written several papers.

The steps in Pascal's thinking rang like pure bell chimes in Claude's head as he stood inside the cathedral. He remembered, he wasn't sure why, the beautiful harmony, the symphony of sound, of the churches of his beloved native county. Dozens of churches across Bedfordshire lent their voices to a rich carpet of sound in the still, balmy air at Christmas time. His mother had wanted him to become a vicar but he had rebelled.

"How are you going to ring the bell with arms like that?" the priest asked Claude abruptly, jolting him out of his reverie.

"I can do it, believe me," said Claude He was desperate to secure the position.

"I bet you can't," said the priest.

"I bet I can," Claude replied. "Let me show you."

They climbed up the many stairs to the bell tower. Claude leaned against a wall, then started running at full speed towards the largest bell. When he struck the bell with his face, it made the most beautiful sound that the priest had ever heard. The sound could be heard not only all over Rubaga Hill, it could be picked up on all of the seven hills of Kampala.

Claude then ran at another bell and with the first bell still resonating, the harmony was magnificent.

He ran again at a third bell, but this time he slipped and instead of hitting the bell he skidded out the bell-tower, through one of the slats, and fell to his death on the ground below.

The priest ran downstairs. A crowd had formed around the dead man's body.

"Who is this *mzungu*?" the crowd asked.

The priest replied, "Well, I don't know his name, but his face rang a bell."

The Bell-Ringer of Montmartre

It's a miracle! The cry went up from the crowd surrounding Claude's body. Despite being pronounced dead by the ambulance men who had arrived, one of his feet was seen to move. Claude had fallen on to a bush in a freshly dug flower bed.

Father Mukasa was delighted. He took pity on Claude and welcomed him into his church. It took Claude months to recover. He was left with such bad injuries, though, that ringing the church bells was out of the question. Father Mukasa encouraged Claude to ring the small bell that is traditionally rung at key moments in the Mass.

Indeed, it was during Mass that Claude glimpsed his way forward. He spoke to Father Mukasa about it and they agreed on a plan. The Church would finance a course on hand bell ringing for Claude. An expert was flown in from London.

Claude took to his course like a duck to water. He worked his way through the syllabus in no time at all: Four Bells, Six Bells, Weaving, Echo, Gyro, Malleting, Martellato, Plucking, Shaking, Singing Bell, Tower Swing, Thumb Damp. Claude was in seventh heaven.

The Vice-Chancellor of Makerere made the charitable decision to allow Claude to continue on full pay as a research fellow until such time as he was back on his feet. Some muttered, "That will be never".

And so his life continued happily in Kampala. He was often to be found in Rubaga Cathedral. Father Mukasa allowed Claude to practice in the vestry. For the priest it was more than an act of charity. He genuinely liked the Englishman. Claude combined an endearing light-heartedness with an engaging seriousness.

However, all was not well in the cathedral. Complaints were beginning to surface that Claude's hand bell ringing could be heard during some services. Father Mukasa asked Claude to tone it down a little but Claude was now so into his new pursuit that things eventually came to a head. Following a phone call to the Head of Music at Makerere, and without Claude being aware of what was going on, he was offered space in one of the tiny practice booths on campus. Students used to gather below the window to enjoy his sweet chimes.

Another cloud began to form on the horizon. One or two bad-natured students began to complain that their access to the booths had been affected by Claude being there too long each day. It came up at the departmental board of studies and, by a narrow majority, it was decided that Claude had to go.

He felt lost. He took to wandering around the city in search of venues. He had by now acquired a suitcase specially designed to take a rack of bells. The only places he found that were vaguely tolerant of his hobby were bars.

He first of all set up shop in the Makerere staff bar. The majority of Claude's colleagues were tolerant of his eccentricity. He would ensconce himself in the games room or in a corner of the bar. Staff would smile as the sweet notes rang out.

Again, he faced another obstacle. A couple of writers, one American, the other from Latin America, were planning a joint talk on the theme of 'The Dignity of the African Good-Time Girl'. They liked to explore such topics. It gave them scope to do field research and data-gathering. They encouraged their students to go out into the city to gain first-hand experience. They were discussing whether the girls they were researching were proto-feminists when their deep thoughts were interrupted by the quiet sound of bells.

The American stared icily at Claude. Claude became aware of the fixed stare coming from the end of the bar. At first, he shook his head. The person did not seem real. He looked like one of those personalised cardboard cut-outs that were becoming popular in Kampala. There was one of a glamorous air-hostess in the East African Airways office in the city centre. A fellow lecturer had purloined it one day by simply walking out with her with his arm round her. She looked so real that nobody raised an eyebrow.

The glaring became more intense. Claude could almost feel the reflected light sparking like electricity from the American's round, steel-framed glasses. There wasn't the slightest twitch of a muscle in the cold, hostile face. At that moment, all Claude was aware of was this menacing, white, emoticon-like white circle emanating ill-will towards him. He packed up his bells and left.

He decided to go and drown his sorrows in Okello's Bar. He took a taxi to the outskirts. Okello's Bar was no more than a tin shack built on bare earth. The earth was swept clean each day and had acquired a shiny look. Claude liked it there. It felt real and Okello liked to welcome wazungu. It wasn't just that he liked their company, which he did, they also made him feel a little safer. Okello showed Claude a machine-gun that he kept under the counter. "They'll try to come and get me one day," he explained to Claude. "I'll be ready." Claude never asked who they were. He wasn't sure but he assumed Okello meant the Baganda. Okello was from the north.

Claude ordered his Tusker and opened up his case. At first, Okello was fascinated by this phenomenon. He liked Claude's version of 'Rudolph the Red-Nosed Reindeer' and Bing Crosby's 'White Christmas'. Englishmen often surprised him with their interests. One of his customers, Alex, a Scotsman, would sometimes fetch his bagpipes from his car. It was good for business. Word would get around and the bar would fill up. Claude began to frequent Okello's bar more and more. Initially, Okello saw that his sales were going up but, after a while, they began to go down. Customers were growing weary of Claude's bells. Okello asked Claude politely but firmly to take his bells elsewhere.

He installed himself in the Gardenia but soon the girls were complaining that their enjoyment of the Animals' 'House of the Rising Sun' and Millie Small's 'My Boy Lollypop' was being ruined by the sound of Claude's bells. The owner tried turning up the volume of the jukebox but it didn't work. He asked Claude to move on, in spite of the fact that Claude was now consuming large quantities of Nile and Tusker.

Claude tried the Rugby Club. He didn't last five minutes. He told me that the mocking words of the song "Why was he born so beautiful, why was he born at all?" were still ringing in his ears as I dropped him off at Mitchell Hall at Makerere.

His next port of call, and what turned out to be his last in Uganda, was the City Bar in the very centre of the town. Claude was totally compos mentis. He knew that his music could irritate people but he just had to practice to keep himself sane. Babu, the owner, was very liberal, very compassionate. He invited Claude to sit out on the veranda at the front of the bar, overlooking Kampala Road. He calculated that the roar of the traffic would mitigate the effect of Claude's bell-ringing.

Now, the country was entering difficult times. Tribalism was raising its ugly head at all levels. The terrace of the City Bar was no longer the safe haven for the weary, the thirsty and the lost that it had been in better times. For example, Melvyn, the barman at the rugby club, who appeared constantly to wear a triumphant smirk on his face - it was, in reality, a product of his embarrassment at his physical ungainliness and his lowly social origin - made the mistake one day of raising his beer glass and grinning at a passing lorry load of soldiers who were clearly from the north. The lorry screeched to a halt. Melvyn dashed for the door at the back, got into his car and shot off before the offended soldiers could find him.

A similar thing happened to Claude. He was tapping away on his bells when a passing Land Rover stopped and an angry officer, a colonel, stepped out. I am not sure what Claude was playing. I have heard that it was 'Ding dong bell, pussy's in the well'. Whatever it was, the soldier heard what he thought was either a subversive tune or an insult. Babu stepped in, placing himself between Claude and the angry colonel. Claude began to pack his case up rapidly. He felt slightly annoyed when he saw Babu tapping his head and nodding towards him.

It dawned on Claude's friends at Makerere, myself amongst them, that Claude was no longer safe in Kampala. The former kind atmosphere of 'live and let live' was fast disappearing. The dictator was beginning to flex his muscles. Even London, it was rumoured, could be reached by his tentacles. Stories were circulating that the king, who had gone into exile in England, may have been poisoned. Paris, it was felt, was becoming the only safe destination for those fleeing the death squads. The staff at the embassy there, who had been in post since the early sixties, had somehow managed to prevent infiltration by hit men. I suggested that Claude be flown to Paris. This was agreed. The authorities at the university said that his salary would be paid to him there, at the Embassy, until he found suitable employment.

Claude loved Paris and Paris took to him. He would sit on a folding chair in the Place du Tertre and play his bells to passing tourists or to people having their portraits done. Coins mounted up in his hat. His crowning achievement was to play in harmony with the bells of the nearby Basilica of the Sacré Cœur. He became known to Parisians as "le Sonneur de Montmartre" and appeared quite often on French TV.

Fate is a funny thing. Claude loved to stand on one of the bridges that cross the Seine by Notre Dame Cathedral. He loved to contemplate the sheer beauty of the building. One New Year's Eve he was there. You could just hear his bells tinkling above the roars of the crowd as they welcomed in the New Year. Rockets went up in the air and the crowd gasped in awe, falling back as they looked up. Claude, who had been drinking heavily, lost his balance and fell over the parapet, still clutching his rack of bells. As he sank into the depths of the river, some say that they swear that they saw a smile on his face and that they could hear him singing: *"I'm ringin' in the Seine / Just ringin' in the Seine / What a glorious feelin' / I'm happy again / I'm laughing at clouds"*. Then, nothing: Claude just disappeared into the icy water.

The Dust Devil Chaser of Amboseli

Owen set out in his Land Rover from a friend's house in Nakuru. He was on his way to the Ecotopia Hotel in Amboseli to discuss his research interests with a colleague from Nairobi. He had nearly completed his journey when his vehicle broke down. He looked out through his side window and saw some elephants ambling by in a cloud of dust.

He loved Amboseli. He knew it well. It was where he did most of his data-gathering. He knew that Amboseli was drying out but, in a curious way, he didn't mind. It was, after all, becoming his bread and butter. He reached for his water bottle. Empty.

"Well," he said to himself, "there is nothing else for it. I shall have to walk." Off he set.

At first he felt he was making good progress. He had a compass and was confident that he was going in the right direction.

Owen Evans's background was Geography. He was proud to have landed a plumb job at Makerere. He had been bored with his work at Swansea University. His work on waterspouts, which could be spotted now and then in the Bristol Channel, had been going nowhere, despite it having taken him to study steam devils – tornadoes over water – on Lake Michigan.

His field of research in Uganda was dust devils. He believed that Uganda would be reduced to a dusty desert within half a century unless people stopped cutting down trees. His PhD topic involved a study of the causes of dust devils, the myths surrounding them, and the names that people around the world gave them. He had just finished doing research among the Kikuyu where, he had found, a dust devil is called ngoma cia aka, which translates as "women's devil" or "women's demon". His research was taking him in the direction of Anthropology and he was pleased about that. He was finding the latter much more interesting than straight, dry Geography.

The discovery of dust devils on Mars had fired his imagination. He felt that he could possibly be moving into an up-and-coming area. He had recently read a paper on the role dust devils had played in around one hundred aircraft accidents. Could they threaten spacecraft, he wondered? He was focusing more and more on the structure and nature of vortices.

As he wandered along across Amboseli National Park, he could not but admire the beautiful shapes of the dust devils that were accompanying him. He felt happy. This was why he was here. His mind went back to a trip he had made to Australia where he had studied Aboriginal myths of the 'willy-willies' or 'whirly-whirlies', as the phenomena are called there. He remembered the story of the spirit that emerged from a dust devil and abducted a child. Children were told this to make them behave.

In many Arabic-speaking countries he had discovered that they were coterminous with djins or genies. Noting that some of those he could see were whirling clockwise, he recalled his great experiences among the Navajo in America. There they are seen as the spirits of the dead. Clockwise spinning indicated a good spirit, anticlockwise ones were bad. In the distance he saw a "bad" one coming towards him.

Lost in these and other thoughts he did not notice how tired he was becoming and how thick the dust was in the air. He began to slow down. By midday, he was on his hands and knees. He was suffering from a terrible thirst. He was finding it hard to breathe.

A man came towards him dressed in traditional Maasai garb.

"Water, water," he cried, pointing his finger into his mouth. "Maji, maji," he repeated in Swahili.

"Hakuna maji," the stranger replied. "No water. Hariri, hariri nzuri." He produced some beautiful silk ties.

"Sitaki hariri tie. I don't want silk ties," he whispered through his parched lips.

The stranger shrugged his shoulders and went on his way.

Clive thought that he had had it. "I'm a 'croaker'", he said to himself, using his native Gower dialect to describe a dead or dying man.

Something in him told him not to give up, that help was near at hand and, lo and behold, in the distance, through the screen of dust, he made out the shape of his destination. He told himself that the first thing he would do, after drinking a gallon of water, would be to jump in its cool, blue swimming pool.

He crawled across the car park watched by a group of horrified Chinese tourists. He headed straight for the restaurant. Dinner was in progress. He was delighted to see that the guests were wearing full evening dress.

"Civilisation!" he said to himself.

"Water," he gasped at a waiter who came towards him. "Reservation." He was unable to form a sentence.

Whether the waiter, who was French-speaking, Tutsi perhaps, did not recognise him or whether he thought that Owen was drunk is not known, but the response he received took away any breath he had left.

"Non, non, monsieur. Pas possible!" the waiter said holding up the palms of his hands as if to stop him. "Vous n'avez pas de cravate. You cannot come in. You have no tie."

The Bowling Green Man of Entebbe

Bob Tell and his wife loved playing bowls. The type of bowls they specifically adored was English lawn bowling. Bob had grown up in a house that overlooked a beautifully manicured bowling green in Luton, England. He had spent many an evening as a child leaning over the fence looking at the bowlers.

He loved the polished wood of their bowls and the sound of bowl striking bowl. For him it was a sort secret language: click-click-click, click, the language of permanence. To him the essential English evening scene was a windless, sunlit green where men and women in whites stood stock-still. It represented stability and respectability, civilisation, Man's mastery of Nature.

Later, when he grew up, he was allowed to join in, despite the fact that he was years younger than the other bowlers.

Then, one day, he was told he had to go to Africa. He was a civil servant and the newly independent country of Uganda needed his area of expertise: agriculture. He was to advise on the best seeds to use in Uganda.

He and his wife, Mary Tell, moved into a bungalow in Entebbe, a short walk from the President's office. Bob liked Entebbe. It was a green and pleasant place. Rain fell regularly on its lawns every afternoon at three. Life was good. The restaurant of the Lake Vic hotel could scarcely be bettered anywhere in East and Central Africa. He understood how Churchill could have called Uganda "the pearl of Africa." But Bob missed his bowling green.

It was then that he decided to do something about it. He decided that what Entebbe needed was a bowls club. There were enough Englishmen and women working in the government offices to make it viable.

He rented from a chief some land near the lake's edge, using money he had inherited from an uncle. He set about flattening his field. He employed a small army of men with wheelbarrows to spread good topsoil garnered from swampy areas that had been drained in Kampala. His mouth watered as the rich black earth went down.

He then had to decide on the grass seed. The grass in Uganda seemed to him to very hard in comparison with the softness of grass in England. He knew through his training that there were grasses that thrived in the cool season and others that were better suited to the warm season, not that these were very distinguishable in the micro-climate at the side of the lake.

Once the field had been flattened and levelled he divided it up into squares. The most successful square would become the green. In one he planted warm season grass seed that was tolerant to drought, i.e. it needed less watering. Water was not his main concern in Entebbe, though, because of the powerful rain storms that built up each day over the lake.

He planted Bermuda grass that, he knew, was quite disease-resistant. He had heard from old Africa hands in the Kampala Club that they tended to use this seed for their lawns. He tried St Augustine grass but realised that it was rather thick-bladed and needed a great deal of water. He experimented with Buffalo grass, very drought-tolerant and needing lots of sunshine.

He did not have much shade at Entebbe and thought that, perhaps, this might prove to be the one. He seeded square after square, one with Zoysia grass, another with Bahia grass, the latter being able to resist most insect attacks. Entebbe was plagued with insects at that time. He tried Kentucky blue grass, fescue grass, tall fescue, which is hard-wearing, red fescue and perennial rye-grass. He was coming to the conclusion that it was this last one that would make the best sward for bowling.

Having set the experiments in motion, he knew he had to just sit back and wait for the results. In one or two cases these could take a year or more. No matter, he installed himself in a wicker chair at the side of his patches and just sat there under a tree smoking his pipe and watching the grass grow.

He became restless. The old urge to play bowls began to reassert itself in earnest. His discussed this with his wife Mary. She understood and approved his plan that they should travel, in their holidays, to established bowling greens in other parts of Africa.

First of all they ventured out to Nanyuki but Bob was not entirely satisfied with the smoothness, or lack of, of the turf. They decided to venture further abroad. They found one that came to love especially, the bowling green in the grounds of Cathedral Peak Hotel in the Drakensberg Mountains of South Africa.

They found another they liked, the Lawn Bowls Club in the Clifton area of Cape Town. Bob was in his element on the South African greens. He didn't really want to go back to Entebbe but, needs must, he and Mary always returned before the end of their holidays.

During one holiday a small clubhouse had gone up, on Bob's instruction, next to one of the squares of land back in Entebbe. This large shed - it wasn't much more than that - became like a second home to Bob. He would sometimes, with Mary's permission, spend the night in it so that he could be up at dawn to put the sprinklers on his rye-grass green. It wasn't ideal but it was the best grass he could come up with. His green was passable.

The years went by and Bob slowly developed an archive in the "club house". In it he kept the records of games: who in Entebbe had got nearest to the jack in 1967, that sort of thing. He and Mary also kept the correspondence they had had with clubs in other parts of Africa. Bob was proud of his archive. It contained newspaper reports of the victories and defeats of the sides he had played for, particularly in Cathedral Peak.

One day the club burned down. No one knows what caused it. Some say that a dispute about the land lay behind it but Bob would never speak about it. He was heart-broken. The fire brigade had cut across his pride and joy, his rye-grass green, carving deep ruts in its surface. It was as if all he had worked for had been defaced, desecrated. And the fact that the paperwork was destroyed in the conflagration means that posterity will never know now for whom exactly the Tells bowled.

The Death's Head Hawk Moth Man of Makerere

Fran Butterworth was having a hard time at Makerere. His research area, 'The Death's Head Hawk Moth', was interesting but he was finding it difficult to enthuse the students who were on his 'Flora and Fauna of Buganda' course. Sometimes he wondered if it was because everything he said was blindingly obvious to anyone who had grown up in the lush Bugandan countryside. He decided to tart his lectures up.

"Do you know, he said, to his somnolent class, that the great English Romantic poet, John Keats, uses the moth as a symbol of death in his 'Ode on Melancholy'.

> No, no, go not to Lethe, neither twist
> Wolf's-bane, tight-rooted, for its poisonous wine;
> Nor suffer thy pale forehead to be kiss'd
> By nightshade, ruby grape of Proserpine;
> Make not your rosary of yew-berries,
> Nor let the beetle, nor the death-moth be
> Your mournful Psyche, nor the downy owl
> A partner in your sorrow's mysteries;
> For shade to shade will come too drowsily,
> And drown the wakeful anguish of the soul.
>
> (Stanza 1)

"What does he mean, sir, by 'mournful Psyche'?"
"Good question, Musaka, Psyche is a genus of moths in the bagworm family, the Psychidae."
"Yes, but ... ."
Fran felt that he might lose control. He also thought he was in danger of getting out of his depth.

"'Psyche' is the name of a mortal woman in Greek mythology, who becomes the wife of Eros."

"That's weird, sir."

"Curiously, it is also the name of a white butterfly", he stuttered.

"No, I mean the association of death with the erotic. Sounds a bit Freudian, sir."

Fran felt beads of sweat forming under his armpits. He decided to take a different tack.

"What do you think of this?" he asked. He produced a reproduction of Van Gogh's 'Death's Head Hawkmoth on Arum'. It was one that he liked and he had it on his wall in his Makerere flat.

Margaret Mubende put her hand up. She was a devout Christian and often tried to bring her main interest in life into any conversation.

"Sir, the lily plays a role in the Christian Easter service as a symbol of Jesus's resurrection. In many paintings the calla lily has been associated with the Virgin Mary or the Angel of Annunciation. It has been linked with holiness, faith, purity and rebirth."

"Very good, Mary," Fran said, not knowing what to reply.

"A bit worrying, then, that image of Van Gogh's. Was he going through a religious crisis?" Kiwanuka called out.

Fran was definitely getting out of his depth.

"Several Death's Head Hawk Moths were found in mad King George III's bedroom. You know the moth can emit a squeak that can really freak anyone suffering from dementia."

"Buñuel and Dalí use it in *Un chien andalou*, sir". Okello was into the avant-garde and was a keen member of the Makerere Film Society.

Fran began to become aware of gaps in his general knowledge.

"It seems to be a reference, in that film, to a son's incest with his mother, sir."

Fran gulped quietly. "This is getting out of hand," he said to himself. He decided to make a break for it.

"Class, let me tell you a story." He looked round to see if the door was closed. He often worried that the Dean, a cadaverous-looking man, might overhear his free-ranging lectures.

"A moth with poor eyesight goes into a podiatrist's office.

'Tell me what your precise problem is,' said the specialist.

'Oh, there is so much. Where do I start?' said the moth.

'Take your time,' the podiatrist said.

'I work all day in a government office in Kampala. I work really hard. No one could work harder but the fact is that I am sure that my boss, the Minister of Agriculture, Animal Industry and Fisheries, seems to be totally unaware of how hard I work. All he does is come in and throw piles of paperwork at me about Nile perch, catfish, tilapia, lungfish, eels and sprat. It seems to give him great pleasure to bury me in documents that he doesn't want to read himself. "Summarise," is all he says.

At night I cannot get to sleep. I wander from one end of the house to the other, like a soul in torment, unable to relax.

I turn to my third wife and look at her. She seems to be ageing as fast as my first two. Sometimes, sitting down for breakfast with the three of them, I feel like fleeing away to another country. I lost my favourite daughter last year to AIDS. My son Paul seems to have less courage to face the challenges of life than I do. I look at him and see myself in him, a coward. If only I had the courage to take my old Enfield rifle out of the cupboard and end it all. I feel like a mosquito stuck in the mesh covering my window next to the nest of spiders in the corner of the frame.'

'Moth, my dear, you are really disturbed. If you don't mind my saying, you ought to go and see Dr Ephrain Kodoki, the Makerere psychiatrist. He is very good. In fact, I think his specialism is this sort of mid-life crisis.'

'Oh!' said the moth. 'Sorry, I thought ... .'

'Tell me,' the podiatrist said. 'Why did you come to see me.'

The moth replied, 'Because the light was on.'"

The class groaned. There were one or two laughs from those worried about their marks. The bell rang. Fran turned to see, briefly, the dark eyes of the Dean's skull-like head.

The Englishman Called Hugh

Three friars were banished from a monastery in Rwanda. They had committed various rule violations, like distilling and illegally selling liquor. The one that had got them into real trouble was their chartreuse noire, which they had been caught exporting to Burundi and the Congo without a licence. They decided to start up a new business altogether, elsewhere.

They travelled around Rwanda looking for opportunities but found nothing. There were no openings in Kigali, nothing in Gisenyi, Butare, Ruhengeri, Kibuye, Gitarama, Cyangugu, Byumba or Gikongoro.

They decided to go to Uganda - one of them spoke English fluently - where they wanted to open up a plant shop. They had an old VW camper van in which they toured around, hoping to spot an opening. They covered the length and breadth of Uganda: Mbarara, Masaka, Fort Portal, Jinja, Soroti, Arua, Mbale and Tororo, eventually deciding that their business could only work in the capital, Kampala.

They rented a shop on Kampala Road. They had opted for selling flowers.

Their business began to prosper. They created a garden centre at Mukono, not far from the capital, where they cultivated roses, carnations, dahlias, marigolds, chrysanthemums, orchids, gingers, heliconias (lobster-claws or false birds of paradise) and asters.

They had suppliers inside Rwanda in Musanze, Nyabihu, Rubavu and Rulindo. Rare plants were brought in surreptitiously by fleeing Tutsis: things were going from bad to worse again inside Rwanda. A trickle was turning into a flood.

They began to specialise in carnivorous plants, especially the Utricularia: the australis, inflexa, livida, raynalii, stellaris, troupini varieties, all found in and imported from Rwanda. Rumours began to circulate that they were conducting experiments in plant gene-splicing in a secret research centre near Entebbe airport, with the aid of a disgraced Makerere academic called Ken.

One day, Mrs Yasmin Bata, from the most exclusive part of Kololo, was shopping at the monks' store, 'Les fleurs du mal', as it was ironically called – one of the monks was a devotee of Charles Baudelaire's poetry. The Aga Khan was coming to visit Kampala and Mrs Bata wanted her house to look better than anybody else's. Her one wish in life at that moment was to be able to entertain His Highness in her luxurious home.

While she was strolling down an aisle with her toddler, a large plant reached out, grabbed her child and ate it. Needless to say, Mrs Bata was upset at the loss of her child. However, the Rwandan brothers refused to believe that one of their plants could have done such a thing.

The woman told all of her friends about the incident at the Jamatkhana and at the Aga Khan High School in Old Kampala, where she was a governor and soon everyone in Kampala was in an uproar. They decided to kick the brothers out of town. An immense crowd of citizens, except for an Englishman named Hugh, a lecturer in Post-Mediaeval English Literature at Makerere, gathered outside the friars' shop, shouting, waving sticks, and demanding that they leave. But the friars said, "No. We're not leaving". So the people gave up and went home.

A couple weeks later, another woman, a Miss Milly Makubuya, a secretary at Makerere University College, who lived on the campus and was having an affair with a Senior Fellow in Development Studies, was walking down Kampala Road looking for flowers with which to decorate the vestibule of the new post-graduate Economics Institute building. The Prime Minister was coming to unveil a bas-relief sculpture of himself, created by a famous Mugandan sculptor out of blackened soapstone. The PM was not a handsome man. To Milly, the face resembled a grotesque death mask, intentionally so, perhaps, she feared and she was exploring the idea that red roses might soften, to some extent, its hideousness. She was also aware that they might also exacerbate its repulsiveness.

Next to the black bas-relief plaque stood the statue of the Institute's founder, Leonard Hull, Len, as everyone on campus affectionately called him. Milly was worried in case the PM took umbrage at the fact his face would be in Len's shade, so to speak. She had debated with herself about whether to cover it up with a sheet or have it temporarily removed. The latter course of action proved not to be possible as she found that it had been screwed securely to the floor.

Len's effigy was as life-like as a Madame Tussaud's waxworks figure. It was life-sized, not very high, about five foot five. Working upwards, one's eye alighted firstly on the bent, gnarled and excessively protruding toes that jutted out from the straps, in concrete, of flip-flops. Thin legs and knobbly knees led one up the shorts, which had a faintly obscene bagginess about them. Above them the sculptor had successfully reproduced the tight see-through shirt with holes in it that revealed that Len had no "pecs". His gaunt face was accurately reproduced with deep ruts running down either side that reminded one of those on the mud road between Uganda and Kenya after a cloud burst. On his head sat a Little Miss Muffet type of circular bonnet. Something had to be done. Neither Len nor the mask was a pretty sight.

She was walking through the friar's shop, looking at plants with her baby, when a plant grabbed her child and ate it. She ran through the streets screaming that a plant had swallowed her baby.

The citizens of Kampala were outraged, and again gathered outside the floral shop (except for Hugh, the post-Mediaevalist), waving torches, and demanding that the friars leave town at once. But the brothers said, "No way" and everyone gave up and went home.

A few days later, yet another woman, a mzungu, Mrs Evangeline Montcroix, the long-serving Secretary of The Kampala Club, who had a fine house on Tank Hill and considered herself to represent the crème de la crème of Kampalan society, dared to take her grandchild into the floral shop. Dame Barbara Cartland had been invited to come and lecture at the club on the theme of 'The affair in the Romantic Novel'. Mrs Montcroix was looking for something exotic with which to decorate the club.

She held her granddaughter tightly in her arms, but it was no use. A large Ficus wrestled the child from her arms and ate it.

When the townspeople heard of this, they were extremely upset. They again gathered outside the friars' shop (except for Hugh), yelling and threatening bodily harm to the friars if they didn't leave town. But the friars said, "We're staying". So, the citizens gave up and began to go home.

Just then, Hugh showed up. He was on his way to Makerere to give a lecture on 'The Relevance of The Canterbury Tales to Post-Colonial East African Society'.

He walked up to the friars, and said, "Get out of town, now!"

The friars immediately packed up all their belongings and fled that very day, never to be heard from again.

Moral: Only Hugh can prevent florist friars.

The Fiendish Uganda Bookshop Plot

Johnny felt very relaxed when his wife left him. He continued to play the field, adding more and more notches to his bedpost. He became indiscreet. He almost welcomed the notoriety he was gaining. His conquests began to talk amongst themselves over coffee in the Uganda Bookshop Coffee House.

His new-found freedom eventually went to his head. He could no longer distinguish between what was acceptable and what was not in the field of human relationships. He became proud of the fact that he was seeing several women all at the same time. He would boast about it openly in the university bar.

His libidinous recklessness began to know no bounds and some whispered that he was showing signs of madness. For example, he announced one day at the Rugby Club that he wanted to show his appreciation to his harem. He wanted to do something that would let them know how much he appreciated them all. He said, with obvious pride, that he was going to take them all on a hot air ballooning holiday in Kenya.

He contacted the company that organises flights over the Masai Mara. The trips, he was told, only lasted an hour but were spectacular. They took off just before dawn. The silence and the peace experienced by balloonists suspended under the multi-coloured canopy were, they said, out of this world. Flights were followed by a champagne breakfast. This was it, he said to himself. He would begin with former girl-friends with whom he felt he was on good terms.

He sent printed invitations to six specially selected young women. In the letter he included airline tickets, money, vouchers and reservations for tents in the camp that was situated next to the launch site.

The day of the treat arrived. The young women were already up and dressed when Johnny arrived in his Land Rover, having spent the night in a comfortable lodge nearby.

As his former girlfriends approached the balloon, Johnny, who was now already in it, called out "Ladies, please step into the basket."

"We are nervous, Johnny," one called out.

"Don't be nervous. It's going to be great," he shouted back, trying to make out their faces in the darkness.

Little did he realise that the 'ladies' had hatched a merciless plan. He did not see what was happening but one of his guests stepped forward with a panga and slashed the rope that was holding the balloon to the ground. Up went the balloon. The sudden movement caused Johnny to pull on the cord that ignited the flame. The balloon shot ever faster skywards.

"Bye, Johnny!" He could just hear their calls as he headed westwards.

Later, back at the camp, spirits were high. The champagne was flowing freely. Toasts were made to the departed lover. They sat there all day, imagining what was happening to Johnny.

"He's over the lions now," Michelle said. "I can just see him frantically throwing out sand-bags to get clear of their claws." Peals of laughter went up.

Later Julie said, "He's over the Owen Falls Dam now, struggling to clear the downdraught that is pulling him into its foaming cauldron." They all fell about giggling.

Even later Wendy spluttered, "He's up in the Rwenzoris, trying to clear the mountain peaks." Tears of mirth were running down their cheeks.

"And now, he is over the Democratic Republic of the Congo and a thousand rebel guns are pointing up at him," said Judy. She was more than a little merry. The group fell silent.

"My God, what have we done?" said Margaret.

A wise old Maasai man who had been eyeing the performance stepped forward.

"Do not worry," he said. "It is not your fault. It is a result of the man's own stupidity. He has got his just reward, his come-uppance. He ignored the advice contained in the time-honoured saying of our forefathers: 'Don't put all your exes into one basket!'"

The Ghastly Soroti Coffin

It was back in the nineteen-sixties. Colin was doing a PhD at Makerere on traditional medicines. He had been investigating the claims of hunter-gatherer tribes-people regarding natural treatments of cancer and had spent years in the forests of Uganda and Zaire quizzing witch doctors and local chiefs. He had not come up with anything positive. If only he could find a berry, a flower, a fruit, any sort of plant with the magic properties he would be made for life. He would become an instant millionaire and not have to work again. His wife might even stay with him. Oh, and yes, he thought, millions of people would be spared a horrible fate.

He had a side-interest. He suffered from an irritating and recurring cough that he put down to something he had picked up in the jungle. He took time off now and then to tour around Uganda trying to track down a local remedy for his cough. He eventually came across one in the north of the country, not far from the Sudanese border. It was the fruit of the sausage tree, Kigelia africana.

It became a bit of an obsession with him. Perhaps it filled the void that the lack of success in finding a cancer cure had left in him.

He packed his flat on the top of Nakasero Hill with the tree's "sausages". He had a frame built in his large kitchen from which he hung the fruit. His kitchen began to resemble a Spanish bar filled with long, dangling hams. Visitors from Karamoja and Achole would often be seen emptying the boots of their cars at the side of the block of flats and carrying armfuls of the fruit to his kitchen door.

He ground up the dried flesh of the pendulous objects and made a sort of tea out of them. This he bottled. By boiling the liquid down, he found he could also make pastilles, cough sweets, if you like, adding sugar and other easily available substances to make them palatable.

He was only too aware that he was running out of funds for his cancer project. The biotech firm in Cambridge that had been backing him was threatening to pull out, leaving him high and dry. He had appealed to the Americans but his pleas fell on deaf ears.

Well, he thought, needs must. He began to travel from town to town in East Africa, selling bottles of his sausage tree cough mixture or packets of tablets to Indian duka wallahs. He began to do a good trade.

He arrived one day in the thriving town of Soroti. Not successful enough yet to stay at the main hotel, he pulled up in the car park of Soroti Club. Somebody had told him they would probably let him sleep on the couch in the bar, if he spoke nicely to the club secretary, Clive Moon.

Colin had great charm and in no time at all he had managed to persuade the secretary to let him sleep in the clubhouse.

They had a few drinks together and then, at about midnight, it was time to turn the lights off and turn in. The secretary locked the door as he left.

Now, in the middle of the bar was a huge coffin. In actual fact it was the bar. What had happened was this. An oversized coffin had been constructed (secretly) by the Public Works Department for a very tall expat who was thought to be dying. However, he went back to UK and died there so it was surplus to requirements. After a few years, no further giants turned up to die so it was given to the club because the PWD needed more space. The unusual bar was the talk of the town.

Colin settled down fully dressed on the sofa. It was quite comfortable and he had a thick blanket under which he could keep himself warm during the cold Ugandan night. He felt secure and fell fast asleep.

Whether it was the alcohol or something else – out of habit he had taken one of his cough drops and perhaps it had reacted with the waragi, the local banana gin favoured by club members – he found himself in the middle of a terrible nightmare.

A strange noise, like a wooden box being moved on the floor, filled the air. The scraping got louder and louder. In his dream he found himself running from one end of the bar to the other, pursued by the giant coffin! He ran to the door to let himself out, only to realise that he was locked in. He tried the windows but they had security devices on them to stop thieves getting in.

Total terror gripped him. He had heard that Clive, whose day job was Head of Biology at Soroti's predominantly Asian high school, had kept huge preserved pythons in the coffin prior to their dissection by the older boys. There was also a rumour circulating in Uganda that mature male gorillas were kept there while waiting for a plane, a de Haviland Dove with extra fuel tanks inside, to come to a secret landing strip outside Soroti whence they were flown away, via a chain of private airfields along the Nile, to private zoos and collectors in Europe and America.

In his dream he experienced the coffin pushing him into the gentlemen's loo. It was crushing him against the old-fashioned urinal. He began to cough. Automatically his hand went into his pocket to locate the small bottle of cough drops.

He took one and immediately the coffin stopped moving. It backed away slightly, enabling him to extract his backside from the bowl. The coughing stopped and the coffin began to slide backwards towards its original position, and function, as the club's bar. The stools that had been knocked over righted themselves.

Then he woke up. He found the light switch. He realised that it had all been a bad dream. He smiled to himself and found himself laughing and singing out loud the following words to the tune of the Andrews Sisters' song 'Money is the root of all evil':

Everybody knows that cough drops stop coughin',
Everybody knows that cough drops stop coughin',
Take them today, take them today, take them today,
Yeah!

The Giraffe Man Among the Twa

Joshua Wetherspoon was a bit of a loner. He was perfectly happy with his own company. This led him to explore the more unusual highways and byways of East Africa.

He was a tall, lanky man. He hailed from the Home Counties town of Bishop Stortford but he was never so happy as when he sitting meditating in a vent on Tororo Rock or investigating the spirits of the Sebei Caves on Mount Elgon.

He developed a fondness for the Twa people of the Bwindi Impenetrable Forest. This was prior to their eviction. He went on to develop an interest in the Great Lakes Twa in general, the Batwa, Abatwa or Ge-Sera, as they are variously called. The tribes in that area were, at that time, relatively under-researched. Joshua felt he had entered an anthropologist's dream, a veritable Wonderland.

The Batwa or Twa are very short people and Joshua towered above them. His Twa hosts would tease him about his extraordinary height, calling him "Mr Giraffe". "Dr Giraffe", he would correct them with a smile. He took their gentle mockery in the spirit it was intended, but, one day, was forcefully struck by what one chief had to say.

"It is not good for you to be so tall," he said. "Just look at your forehead. It is covered in scars and cuts. You need to be smaller. Then you will be able to follow us more quickly as we hunt animals and gather fruit in the forest."

"What do you suggest?" asked Joshua in Kirundi, the language his friends had adopted.

The chief produced a bottle containing a liquid. He called it the Shrinking Potion.

"Like the one in Alice in Wonderland?" Joshua said, holding the bottle up to the light.

"We have not heard of this Alice," said the chief.

"I have," said a small child cheekily, putting up his hand. He was attending the nearby primary school.

Joshua decided to give it a go. He had become strangely self-conscious working among the Twa. If it worked, he would, he felt, fit in better. He would not be quite so conspicuous.

He took the bottle back to Makerere where he asked technical staff in the Medical Faculty lab to analyse its contents for anything dangerous. He didn't want to ingest anything hallucinogenic. It would not have gone down well in his lectures on African Anthropology if he had started hallucinating in front of the students.

"All clear," came the reply from the lab. Joshua started to take the medicine.

It was one of his students who first noticed that he seemed to be losing height.

"Are you all right, sir? You seem to be shrinking," one remarked.

"I am fine," he replied, smiling contentedly.

Secretly, he was happy with the effects of the potion. He began to take larger doses. His height shot down. Over a period of about six months he went from six foot seven to four foot one. He began to take more and more. The concoction was beginning to prove addictive. He couldn't stop. By now he was down to three foot. He began to panic. The experiment, he realised, was spinning out of control.

Swallowing his pride – he hated to admit ever that he was wrong - he decided to pay a visit to the campus doctor. He had heard from his students that Dr Patel was very good.

He sat in the waiting room. All eyes were on him. Nobody had seen a three foot mzungu before. He became terribly self-conscious and decided that he could bear it no longer. He had to jump the queue.

He stood up and went over to the surgery door.

"Dr Patel, I must see you NOW!" he shouted.

Dr Patel called out that he was with a patient.

"No, now, Dr Patel, I must see you immediately," Joshua pleaded through the closed door.

The door opened. Dr Patel eyed him up and down.

"I am sorry, Dr Wetherspoon," he said. "As I said, I am with a patient. I am half-way through removing a jigger from his toe."

"But ... ," spluttered Joshua.

"No I am sorry, Dr Wetherspoon," Dr Patel insisted. "You'll just have to be a little patient."

The Glutton of Namirembe

Dave Smiley was a nice chap. He was an Economic Historian. He had a flat up near Namirembe Cathedral where he was regular worshipper.

At first everything went well for Dave in Kampala. He was a good-looking young man with an easy manner and was popular with the ladies. In fact, he began to acquire a reputation for being "a bit of a ladies' man". In Dave's case this was not frowned upon. He treated all of his girlfriends with respect and affection and very rarely two-timed them.

Prior to occupying his flat he had lived in a hall of residence at Makerere. Colleagues noticed that he was becoming overfond of the mainstay of the canteen, matoke. Unlike most of his friends, Dave took a liking to what was, in essence, mashed banana. He rubbed his hands together gleefully each time it was served up, which was most days. It came with chunks of tough, tasteless, gristly meat and thin, flavourless gravy.

When he moved into his flat, he employed a young Ugandan woman, Florence, to come in and prepare his favourite meal: garlic and cumin matoke. He loved the look of it and its soft, silky feel. He became a connoisseur of matoke, which he would often say should be spelt matooke. He would sally forth on a Saturday morning to local markets in search of the best green bananas.

Nobody is quite sure when his trouble started. Some say it was when he developed a taste for grilled snake. He enjoyed the whole range of tastes of snake meat, which went from chicken to fish. He became so knowledgeable about snake that he could tell the difference between the cooked flesh of the Egg-eating Snake, the Green Mamba, the Black Mamba, the Gabon Viper, the Puff Adder, the Rock Python, the Green Tree Snake, the Mole Snake and the Boom Slang.

He went on to become an expert in identifying the bush meat that was served up at roadside barbecues near Makerere: bat, monkey, rat, impala. One of his favourites was zebra, which he found to be sweeter than beef.

Money was no object when it came to feeding his meat-eating habit. He was known to travel down on more than one occasion to Mick Nolan's Safari Lodge in Northern Rwanda for the Irishman's eland steaks. To Dave eland tasted better than the best prime fillet steak.

Some say that the real trouble began as a result of reading a passage from a first, early draught of a famous book on Buganda written by a friend of his, *A Night in Buganda*. The passage went like this: "I have never had a curry since that was better than that served by Babu in the City Bar Restaurant. The side dishes, for a start, were out of this world, a meal in themselves: pineapple, coconut, tomatoes, cucumber, relish, banana, sultanas, paw-paw, peppers, the list went on and on. I understand that the cuisine was basically Gujarati and had evolved into something more local. I didn't need to go any further."

Dave was hooked. Starting at the City Bar, he began to explore the rich world of Indian cuisine in earnest. He came to know every Indian curry house in Kampala and beyond. He began to cultivate friendships with his Indian neighbours in order to be invited out for a meal with them. He discovered with delight that his cook had once worked for the Madhvanis on one of their tea plantations.

He loved everything Indian: hot samosas, tandoori chicken, vegetable jalfrezi, paneer tikka masala, naan, chicken razala, aloo gobi, daal baati chuma, amritsari kulcha, the lot. For over a year you would find him guzzling down curries in the city's eateries: bhunas, biryanis, dhansaks, dopiazas, jalfrezis, kormas - especially kormas - madrases, moghul masalas, pasandas, rogan joshes, saags and vindaloos, you name it, they were all grist to his glutinous mill.

All this time he failed to notice that his collars and trousers were beginning to feel too tight. He went from a fifteen inch collar to an eighteen and a half in one year. Even his forty-four inch waist trousers were starting to feel uncomfortable.

He did eventually become aware of this growing problem and on one visit to his parents in Hampstead Garden Suburb took the opportunity to visit a shop for outsized men that used to be halfway down Camden High Street in London. As you drove up from Mornington Crescent you could see the advert high up on the wall of the store, on your right. It said in huge letters, "Alfred Kemp can fit anyone".

From being an attractive male he was turning into an unattractive one. This did not bother him. He had lost his svelte looks, and that physical nimbleness that had made him such a handy scrum-half and accurate feeder of the ball at the Rugby Club. The National Theatre had stopped asking him to play the Beast in their annual production of Beauty and The Beast. Young ladies had stopped knocking uninvited on his door.

On one occasion, he had incurred the wrath of the dictator when four colleagues mockingly carried him on an old door around the rugby pitch after a drinking session in which Dave had consumed fifteen pints of Bell lager. Amin let it be known that he was not amused. It was his, the dictator's, party trick. However, because rugby was involved, which Amin loved, nothing came of it.

Some argued that Dave, "Smiler", as his close friends called him, was responding deep down to a growing tension in the country. Word had got about that the dictator, claiming that the idea had come to him in a dream, was constructing concentration camps in the north of the country in which to incarcerate the Indian population. Perhaps this explained the urgency with which Dave set about satisfying his culinary cravings. Later that year the owners of his much-loved eating places were given ninety days to leave the country. The deadline was the eighth of November, 1972. Dave's eating spree went into overdrive.

Then there was nothing. The restaurants closed down. Even his cook had gone into hiding because of her connections with her former Indian employers. You could say it came as a wake-up call to Dave. He looked into the mirror one day and saw himself as he really was, as he had become, that is.

He decided that he had to go and see someone. He went to the university campus doctor, Dr Mair, a Scotsman. Dr Mair was under enormous pressure because Uganda had suddenly lost most of its doctors. His patience was at breaking-point. Dave explained why he had come, although that would have been obvious to anyone with eyes in his head to see.

The doctor took one look at him and said in an off-hand way, "I can't help ". He turned away.

"I beg your pardon?" said Dave.

"It has gone too far. You are super morbidly obese. Your organs will have been fatally damaged." He said this with his back to Dave.

Dave was outraged by the doctor's abrupt manner. He exploded.

"I DEMAND a second opinion!" he shouted.

"A second opinion? You want a second opinion?" Dr Mair replied dismissively and with a "huh".

"You can have one. You are HIDEOUS!"

The Hills of Uganda

It was a dark and stormy night. Fred Hill and his new wife Betty were driving along a dark Lane near Oxford. They had come to visit a relative at the nearby nursing home.

They were very tired, having just got back from Uganda where they had been involved in sorting out the possessions of a relative at Makerere who had just been rescued from an Amin gaol. They had stayed on in their relative's house on the university campus after he had gone. At times they had wondered if they would have been swept up in the aftermath and might have not managed to return home to the UK.

Amin had been threatening to have their relative shot for having insulted him in a book. It had taken the Prime Minister, the Queen and even the President of Zaire to secure his release. The boot of the car contained a boxful of the offending books that they planned to take a second-hand bookshop in Oxford.

It was late and raining very hard. Fred could barely see the road in front of the car. Suddenly, the car skidded out of control! Fred attempted to control the car, but to no avail! The car swerved and smashed into a tree right opposite the Modern Life nudist colony.

Moments later, Fred shook his head to clear the fog. Dazed, he looked over at the passenger seat and saw his wife unconscious, with her head bleeding! Despite the rain and the unfamiliar countryside, Fred knew he had to get her medical assistance. He carefully picked her up and began trudging down the road. After a short while, he saw a light. He headed towards the light, which was coming from a large, old house. A sign said "BUPA: Bullingden House".

He approached the door and rang the bell. A minute passed. Duncan, whose wife was a patient in the home, opened the door.

The carers were busy and shift change time was approaching. A doctor called in only once a week.

Fred immediately blurted out, "Hello, my name is Fred Hill and this is my wife Betty. We've been in a terrible accident, and my wife has been seriously hurt. Can I please use your phone?"

"I'm sorry," replied Duncan, "but we don't have a phone. Reception is closed. But my friend is a doctor. Come in, and I will get him!" Fred brought his wife in. An older man came down the stairs.

"I'm Bob. I'm afraid my friend may have misled you. I am not a medical doctor; I am a PhD. My wife is a resident here. However, it is miles to the nearest A&E and I had some basic medical training on the DipEd course at Makerere in Uganda. I will see what I can do. Duncan, bring them into the TV room opposite the kitchen."

"Makerere!" Fred gasped. He was amazed at the coincidence but he was too shattered to explain.

With that, Duncan picked up Betty and carried her down the corridor, with Fred following closely. Duncan placed Betty in a chair in the TV room. Fred collapsed from exhaustion and his own injuries. Duncan placed him down on the thick carpet.

After a brief examination, Duncan's friend Bob looked worried.

"Things are serious, Duncan. Prepare a transfusion."

Duncan bared his arm and the two of them worked feverishly with a tube they had found by the nurses' station, but to no avail. Fred and Betty Hill were no more.

The Hills' deaths upset Duncan's friend Bob greatly. Wearily, he walked to the other TV room, which houses an electronic piano. For it was here that he had always found solace. He began to play, and a stirring, almost haunting melody filled the house.

He liked to put his poems to music but on this occasion he needed to sing a song that first echoed around the corridors of the halls of residence at Makerere in Uganda in 1966, 'The

Woman from Guantánamo' ('Guantanamera'), inspired by José Martí's poem. It would, he felt, revive his spirits. He began in English.

I am a truthful man
From where the palm tree grows
And before dying I want
To let out the verses of my soul
Guantanamera, Guantanamera lady.

Having finished the three other stanzas of the song and doubling the volume on the electronic keyboard, he launched into the better known, Spanish, version of 'Guantanamera':

Yo soy un hombre sincero
De donde crece la palma
Y antes de morirme quiero
Echar mis versos del alma
Guantanamera, guajira Guantanamera.

Meanwhile, Duncan was still in the other room tidying up. It normally annoyed him when Bob sang in Spanish but on this occasion there was something different. His eyes caught a movement and he noticed the fingers on Betty's hand twitch, keeping time to the haunting piano music. Stunned, he watched as Fred's arm began to rise, marking the beat! He was further amazed as Betty and Fred both sat up straight!

Unable to contain himself, he dashed down the corridor into the TV room with the piano.

He burst in and shouted to his friend:

"Bob, Bob! ... The Hills are alive with the sound of music!"

The Kampalan Clairvoyant

Young David had not had much success with women. After several months of loneliness as a lecturer in Maths in Kampala, he finally met the one he had been looking for - Lorraine. She taught PE at Gayasa High School. He called her Lorrie. She called him Dave.

Several happy weeks went by for Dave. He and Lorrie were perfect together, he felt. He loved her face, her sense of humour, everything about her was just right. She moved in with him, much to the annoyance of her headmistress.

Six weeks into their budding relationship things were already beginning to look a little less perfect. Lorraine was becoming impatient with some of Dave's interests: collecting East African beer bottle labels, coins and stamps. She could not appreciate how he loved doing things she viewed as infantile. She even began to rage against his huge collection of pop records, threatening to destroy 'My Boy Lollipop' one night when he was playing it on his personal jukebox, that he had had imported specially from America. (He had previously enjoyed playing the jukebox in The Gardenia but that place was out of bounds now that he was a married man.) It would have involved, she had thought, putting a golf club through the glass. She particularly disliked it when he took out his guitar and started imitating Bob Dylan. It sounded to her like caterwauling.

Dave, meanwhile, could not understand Lorraine's obsession with trying to make him dress differently. What was wrong with Airtex shirts, baggy shorts and flip-flops?

One night, Dave was out on the town with the lads in Kampala, when he happened to meet another young lady by the name of Claire-Lee. It was at the New Life Club. He was a little inebriated, and found himself flirting with the pretty girl, almost forgetting Lorraine. He ordered her a Tusker and together they scrutinised the label, looking for a printing error that could make it valuable, whilst a cacophony of Congolese music to which they were oblivious, ground on and on like a hurdy gurdy in the background.

Claire-Lee, it turned out, was every bit as geeky as Dave. She collected Belgian beer bottles, cheese labels from around the world, pictures of the British royal family and American cigarette packets. He found the time with her flying by as they chatted about their latest finds.

Eventually, the lights in the club came on. His friends had already gone so Dave offered to drive Claire-Lee home in his battered old Beetle. She accepted. He got out of the car to open her door and they walked together towards her hut. They said goodnight and Claire-Lee startled Dave as she pulled him to her for a goodnight kiss. Before he left, she took his wrist and wrote her phone number on his arm with her favourite fuschia lipstick.

The next morning, Dave awoke with a bit of a hangover. The hornbill outside the window was playing on his nerves. He felt a little guilty about chatting Claire-Lee up and kissing her, but, well, nothing had really happened.

He resolved to tell Lorraine all about it to assuage his feelings of guilt. Surely she would understand? She didn't. It was the last straw. She told him she didn't want to see him anymore. She needed space. He was stifling her. They were breaking up. She went back to England, to her parents' house in Leeds, breaking her contract in the process. Dave heard rumours that she joined the YIP, the Yorkshire Independence Party.

She left a sad Dave alone in his Nakasero flat, except for the buzzing mosquitoes. He realised it had been inevitable, they didn't share common interests, but it was still painful. Then he looked down at his arm, at the number scribbled there. And he realised something. Something that made him happy. So happy that he grabbed his guitar and burst into song, singing so loud that the neighbours would have heard:

> *I can see Claire-Lee, now Lorraine has gone,*
> *I can see all obstacles in my way;*
> *Gone are the dark clouds that had me blind.*
> *It's gonna be a bright (bright), bright (bright)*
> *Sun-Shiny day.*

The Music Man of Kololo

Johnny was a lecturer in Economics at Makerere. Before coming to Uganda he had lectured in pop music at a college in London. He had a soft spot for the ladies. He had a beautiful wife but he just couldn't help himself.

He and his wife had, he thought, a great deal in common. They loved pop music. It was the sixties and new records were coming out each week. He and his wife would head down from their house on Kololo to the music shop in the centre of Kampala and buy the latest release from the Beatles, the Rolling Stones, The Who, The Hollies, The Beach Boys and the Monkees. He particularly liked The Monkees. Johnny not only sang their songs out loud at home, he could be heard chanting them in his office. He and Cheryl even developed a system of communication made up of catch phrases and memorable lines from pop lyrics. Cheryl was merely humouring him. She did not his share his taste in music but she felt she could keep him by pretending to do so.

Whenever Johnny saw a pretty face he just melted. He was becoming seedy. Cheryl was aware of his weakness. He hardly concealed it from her. Needless to say, she was not happy about it, although she did her best not to show her unhappiness. She bottled up her feelings.

They attended Kampala Folk Club meetings. Johnny would place himself on a sort of counter in the room from where he could survey the faces of those seated. Cheryl sat beside him. He liked the club even though he disliked traditional British folk music. He found it boring and repetitive. He didn't particularly like the beards and sandals dress code. The ladies, of course, did not have beards. Johnny would often sit facing Julie from Leeds. Her husband was neglecting her and he knew he could easily catch her eye. He did. During a pause for drinks he arranged to meet her on the old Kololo air strip.

The Makerere Jazz Club was another place he frequented. He adopted the same procedure, this time managing to catch the attention of Lucy, whose father was an important entrepreneur in the city. He owned the main supermarket. Johnny contrived to meet her in the Baháʼí Temple.

The university bar did not provide rich pickings. Most of the regulars there were men. However, Johnny knew that while the men were there, their pretty wives were at home and he was not opposed to dropping in on them unexpectedly.

Not that Johnny gave himself exclusively to English women. His research involved visits to French-speaking countries of Africa and this gave him an entry into events at the French Embassy. For these he would wear semi-formal dress code. He felt less inhibited at these functions and would be drawn to comely faces like a moth to a candle.

He was very discreet about these adventures. He did not boast about them at the Rugby Club. The latter proved to be a tougher nut to crack. The wives there tended to hide the light of their beauty under a bushel, deliberately dressing down in an unattractive way and abandoning make-up. Many wanted to fit in and be seen to be one of the lads. Johnny didn't like going to club parties very much for the reasons given above. Notwithstanding, he did spot one flower and it is said that he kissed her after a game round the back of the clubhouse while the men were in the showers. Johnny tended to make excuses when asked to play, in order to keep himself available, *disponible*, as he used to stay.

As I said, he tried to be careful, at least when in Kampala. In Nairobi he was shameless. He was blatant in his approach to attractive women at The Starlight Club. He would simply walk up to them and announce that he found them beautiful. He particularly sought out air-hostesses who worked for East African Airways.

His most daring exploits involved ladies from the Asian community. He would engineer invitations to night-long music events. He would sit unobtrusively facing the sitar player and as if by accident would exchange subtle glances with women of his choice. He tended not to pursue such ladies so often, as he found that he was knocking up expensive hotel bills, often in out of the way game lodges.

And so it went on. Johnny was quite happy with the set-up. He had convinced himself that men are not monogamists. He failed to notice that his wife was becoming increasingly uncomfortable with his behaviour. She was, in fact, near breaking point.

Johnny had spent that particular Saturday afternoon playing over and over again the latest Monkees album, Instant Replay. Cheryl picked up the cover. She hated the way the Monkees dressed. She threw it down.

"What are you doing!" Johnny gasped, swinging round to face her.

"I hate the Monkees. I can't bear them. I am leaving you. You'll be able to spend all your days and nights listening to their ridiculous, adolescent songs." She left him, going back to her mother in Bromley.

"What happened?" Mike asked at high table at Makerere some days later. Mike's field was Sugar.

"It's most peculiar, Mike," Johnny said, "She said she was leaving me over my enthusiasm for the Monkees!"

"What!" said Mike, surprised.

"Yes, it's strange. I didn't believe her at first but then I saw her face."

The Lord of Nyamuliro

Patrick had had a bad start. He was extremely bright but had rebelled violently against the middle class life style of his family in Buntingford where his father was the local doctor. After several disastrous adventures in the Middle East and North Africa, he settled into a teaching job in a small, private school near Mubende. He was not qualified.

It was there that his innate inventiveness first began to blossom. He invented a ping-pong table that also served as a door. It had two parts that could be lowered into different rooms, one player in one room, the other in the other. He devised a strange duck bill-shaped contraption to go over his dog's nose together with a gadget in it for turning a bark into a quack. His pride and joy was a full body contraceptive to combat the AIDS epidemic then sweeping the country. Female staff would back away from him when he tried to explain how it worked. He wrote to medical firms in the UK and America but got no response. Other inventions of his included metal detecting sandals. a motorcycle powered water pump - mobile of course - and a loo roll antitheft chain with lock.

His Mugandan wife Winifred saw the potential in him. She urged him to branch out, to be more ambitious. Perhaps, she calculated, he might one day strike it rich.

He toured the palm tree garages on the outskirts of Kampala. Sheets of metal could be picked up at rock-bottom prices. There was a car breaker on the Kampala to Entebbe Road who dismantled cars that had been in a crash and could not be economically repaired. He acquired good sheets of metal that he could beat into different shapes behind his small house.

One project he had nursed for some time was to create a flying machine. Using a motorbike engine he fashioned an aircraft that resembled a powered glider. He had always felt a fear that he might one day have to make a rapid escape, to make a run for it from wherever he was. It was like a form of paranoia. His experiences in North Africa and Syria may have been behind that.

He constructed a narrow runway that ran down a slope in the school grounds. He kept his powered glider at the ready under banana trees at the top end of the runway. As far as is known, it never flew. Some said he never got round to building it. They said he had got carried away when watching James Stewart, Richard Attenborough and Peter Finch in 'The Flight of the Phoenix' in the Kampala Odeon at the end of 1965. Others said that he was haunted by a sense of guilt and a dread of being caught up with after running into a herd of cows on the unmade earth road between Uganda and Kenya. He hadn't stopped.

This much is known: during his spare time he spent a year on the edge of Lake Victoria attempting to create a craft that was propelled by a motor with a propeller on a pole. He used a traditional Ugandan canoe for the venture but only succeeded in going round and round in circles on the water.

Civil War broke out in Uganda. It raged ferociously in the Luweero Triangle where Patrick, his wife and daughter had their home. The school at which he taught was overrun by soldiers one day and was left in smoking ruins. Patrick and his family fled to the south of the country, to an area that had suffered some deprivation but was peaceful.

They arrived, then, in a small village at the bottom of a hill, well away from armed conflict. Patrick became an authority on bee-keeping, There was some economic activity in the area the area owing to the presence of a wolfram mine but the latter was in danger of closing. The little bit of money that Patrick had saved would go a long way there. He could afford a nice grass hut, the best there was then, in Nyamuliro.

Patrick sensed the power that his money gave him. People came to him for small amounts that he was well able to hand out. Soon villagers were bringing him chickens, eggs, tomatoes, everything. He began to live like a lord. The locals encouraged him in this for they saw that the vainer he became, the more likely he was to bestow largesse. Patrick gave generously. He became known far and wide in Kigezi for his munificence, for his charity, his philanthropy. The unexpected arrival of a small inheritance from an aunt in Colchester only served to boost his reputation. His fame even spread to the nearby towns of Kisoro and Kabale where he became a source of gossip in the clubs.

He called together what he described as his personal court or kitchen cabinet. He felt that he had by now practically achieved the status of local chief. The actual chief did not seem to mind. He was shrewd and he knew he could milk the situation. He sat next to Patrick at these meetings, nodding vigorously in agreement whenever he could. Patrick asked one day what could be done to underline his importance. He wondered whether a moat would be in order. He had seen an advert for a floating "Stockholm" duck house in a copy of a UK paper sent out to him. It was pointed out that a moat would attract mosquitoes.

"A throne, bwana, a throne. We should make you a magnificent throne!"

Patrick nodded sagely and so it came to pass: a wonderful ceremonial chair was ordered for Patrick. Exiled wood carvers from Rwanda were employed. They gave the chair a certain tall, high, Tutsi and aristocratic look. Patrick took to sitting in it proudly every day. It sat in the centre of his large hut.

This new feeling of importance led to Patrick to make a mistake. He began to voice criticism of certain figures in the president's court. Warning bells rang in the real village chief's head and he tried to point out to Patrick the error of his ways but he would have none of it. He was still smarting, deep down, at the rough treatment that had suffered in his former home near Mubende. The chief feared trouble.

One day his wife complained that she could not clean underneath it very well and, anyway, it took up too much room. She had had to move their bed too near to a window. The throne had to be moved, she said.

Patrick sat for days contemplating the problem. He did not want to displease his wife. Nor did he want to lose the aura of majesty, power and augustness that he felt the chair bestowed on him. From it he could see right down the path to the rest of the village and he knew that the sight of him sitting there in regal splendour inspired awe and reverence in his "courtiers", most of whom were laughing up their sleeves at him. Still, he was after all the village's main source of income.

One morning he had a light bulb moment. His power of invention, that had been neglected for some time, came back. He looked up into the high roof of the hut and saw solid beams of wood. He would have a pulley attached to a crossbar between the vertically converging beams. One or two of the men working at the mine were good with ropes and pulleys. The Norwegian owner of the mine, a kindly man called Harold, let him have some equipment for free. Mining had practically ground to a halt, as wolfram prices worldwide had plummeted.

This is what he did: he had ropes and chains attached to the four legs of his throne. At night men would come in to hoist the bed up into the roof. It would be secured by a man on a ladder. Then the ropes were moved and attached to Patrick's bed that was left hanging up in the roof area during the day. Patrick felt he was living the life of Riley.

One day the conflict that had gripped the Luweero Triangle flowed south. Early one morning soldiers swept through the village. They charged into Patrick's house, ordering him and his wife out of bed. His daughter was staying with relatives in Kampala. One of the men fired his gun into the air. A bullet hit one of the ropes, severing it. The throne tipped to one side and then came crashing down, narrowly missing everybody, apart from Patrick. He was terribly injured and, cutting a long story short, he, his wife and daughter left Uganda as soon as he was fit enough, taking refuge in Boston, America. To this day the elders of that village shake their heads and repeat the maxim: "People in grass houses should not stow thrones".

The Man with an Orange Head

Business was good for Babu, the owner of The City Bar in Kampala. Expats throughout the country had decided it was going to be their number one watering hole in Uganda. It was the place they all headed for when they had some leave. They descended on it from far and wide - from Moroto and Mbarara, Kasese and Kabong, Arua and Mbale.

One day Babu was cleaning the top of the bar when a strange-looking person walked in. He, the customer, was wearing a Savile Row suit and had a beautiful model on each arm. Each of the women, he explained, were Ugandan princesses. "Their father has fallen on hard times," he whispered. Babu looked past him at the gleaming pink Cadillac parked outside. There was just one thing, though, the man had a head that looked remarkably like an orange: very orange, smooth, deep pores but with barely visible main features.

The new arrival sat down at the bar and called out in a loud voice, "Drinks on me." He peeled off several one hundred shilling notes from a roll of hundreds and managed to get the attention of every man and, the important thing for him, woman in the bar, despite having an orange for a head.

Babu, the owner and bartender, was a discreet man. You could trust him with your innermost secrets, even your financial ones. People had so much faith in him that he acted as a sort of unofficial banker to those expats who were not careful enough with their money for the official banks' liking. Babu did not want to pry but his curiosity now got the better of him and he began to ask about the man's life.

"Excuse me," he said, "but I can't help but notice that you're obviously incredibly wealthy and irresistible to women, but, how can I put it, you have an orange for a head. How did that happen?"

So the man told his story. "A little while ago, when I was practically penniless, I was walking along the beach in Entebbe, turning my problems over in my mind, and I saw a metal object, half-buried in the sand. The price of wolfram, tungsten, you know, the stuff I mine, used to make missiles, had sunk to an all-time low and I was finding it hard to retain my workers at my mine in Kigezi. I simply didn't have the wherewithal to pay them. I even had to open the cages of my private zoo. There was no one left to feed the animals apart from me. My wife had left me and had gone back to Cyprus. I had even had to take up a part-time post as a technician in the Metallurgy Department at Makerere.

Anyway, lost in these thoughts and feeling very sorry for myself, my foot suddenly struck, as I said, a metal object sticking up out of the sand. I picked it up and began to clean it. It was a lamp. I kept on cleaning it, using spit and my shirt sleeve, when Whoosh! out popped a genie."

He took a sip of his Nile. Babu produced another bottle from under the counter.

The whole bar suddenly went silent. You could hear a pin drop. Play was suspended at the pool table. Cues were placed against the walls. The regulars from Makerere gathered round in a small circle, admiring the man's suit and his glamorous companions. Babu made a disapproving sign with his head to Frank Maurice, a mature, post-grad DipEd student at Makerere, signaling that he was getting too near to one of the young ladies. The rich newcomer wiped the beads of perspiration running down the orange skin of his head.

"The genie explained that he had been the possession of an Arab slave trader whose boat had been caught in a sudden squall on Lake Victoria. The vessel had gone down near the Ssese Islands off Entebbe. He had been stuck in the lamp for two hundred years. He said that he was incredibly grateful to me for freeing him that I could have three wishes: anything, anything at all that I desired.

For my first wish I asked him for as much money as I could ever want or need. The genie said, 'It is done!' From then until now, whenever I have needed money, it has been there, in my wallet.

For my second wish I asked for the attention of all the most beautiful women in the world. The genie said it was done, and since then I have been able to get any woman I wanted: Asian, African or European." The two African princesses sitting either side of him giggled.

"For my third wish - and, this is the bit where I sort of messed things up. I don't know why. If you like, you could quote the Latin proverb *Capra Scyria*, the goat that is said to kick over the pail after being milked. That's in Erasmus's A*dagia*. It's not an unusual human trait. Perhaps it was because of a trace, a residue, of a childhood naughtiness, or a deep, innate rebelliousness, a certain 'diablerie', devilment, or 'méchanceté', as they say in the Congo. Or was it related to a feeling that this was all too good to be true? I don't know. Perhaps the devil did get into me at that moment, a British feeling that disaster must surely lie around the corner. Perhaps I was just testing the genie to see if he was no more than an automaton and did not really have my best interests at heart. Perhaps it was my English ego-bursting sense humour. Was I making fun of the genie? I don't know, I don't know what it was. I just don't know what got into me."

"But what happened?" asked Babu.

"I asked the genie for an orange for a head."

The Missionaries of Bujumbura

Brian and I had agreed to smuggle two American teachers out of the country. Their school in Kampala had just erupted in riots and they were in deep trouble. They told us their lives were in danger.

I am afraid I took advantage of the situation. I argued that the safest route would be to go from lake to lake. I had always wanted to see the lakes of Rwanda. Someone had told me it was the Switzerland of Europe. As it turned out, it proved to be the safest way, because the one time we went back onto the main road, we were stopped and forced to stand up against a wall by some nervous soldiers wielding machine guns as they searched the car. It was not a nice experience.

We entered Rwanda at Gatuma and headed towards Lake Kivu, following the scenic route. I had already drawn up the itinerary. The other places I dearly wanted to see were Lake Ruhondo, Lake Mugesera, Lake Burera, Lake Muhazi, Lake Ihema and Lake Cyohoha South.

You could say that our itinerary followed the craziest, most zigzagging and looping route imaginable but it was worth every minute of it, as view after breathtaking view came into sight. The astonishing thing was that we were in the most crowded country in Africa, possibly in the world, and there seemed to be no one around.

We arrived safely in Burundi. Our two passengers caught their plane to America and, mission accomplished, we went into town to relax. We booked into a hotel and decided to find a good restaurant. We found one almost opposite the Hotel Liberté.

It was like a mirage, an oasis in the darkness. The lights were out in Bujumbura, except for those of the restaurant. It had huge plate glass walls and a brightly lit terrace. We decided to eat outside. I went in to talk to the manager while Brian sat down to peruse the menu.

Brian's eyes were popping out of his head. Escargots bourguignonne, champignons Portabella aux quatre fromages, soupe à l'oignon, carré d'agneau, poulet à la provençale, tarte tatin, soufflé au Grand Marnier, profiteroles au chocolat - the list went on and on.

Sitting there, illuminated by the bright spotlights on the outside wall, he cut a fine figure. Tall and athletic, his blond, curly hair caught the light and gave him the appearance, I suppose, of a Greek god, an Alexander resting by the Indus, despite the broken nose and cauliflower ears - the legacy of years of playing number eight in the scrum.

A crowd began to form. Armed with schoolboy French Brian was delighted to hear the phrase "Ce sont des missionaires". Brian was a good sort, with a generous heart, but the last thing he would have called himself was a missionary. He was saving up to buy a house in the UK. Nevertheless, he found the whispering flattering. He beamed at his admirers and gave them the occasional regal wave. He ordered his meal, *steak frites* and *tarte tatin* and a bottle of good red beaune, a Domaine des Croix, Bressandes 1er Cru 1962.

I came outside having ordered my meal at the bar. I had the *escargots, bœuf bourguignonne* and *poire belle Hélène*. I had noticed the crowd forming outside but had not given it a second thought, until I sat down and tuned in to what they were saying. I heard a mixture of Swahili and French.

The first phrase I heard alarmed me: "Yeye zeruzeru?" (Is he an albino?) They were pointing at Brian's tight curls. It worried me because I had heard hair-raising stories concerning the fate of albinos in nearby Tanzania. I decided to ignore it. The crowd continued to grow.

Brian was beaming with contentment. He had finished off his soup and was tucking in to his steak and chips with great relish.

"Did you hear that, Bob?" he asked.

"What?" I said.

"Listen."

I stopped eating and tried to make out what was coming from the onlookers.

"You see, Bob? Ce sont des missionaires. They think we are missionaries." I listened carefully.

"No, Brian, they are saying 'Ce sont des mercenaires'. They think we are mercenaries! Run for it!"

The Naked Woman in the Kampala Odeon

An Ecumenical Conference of Catholics and Anglicans was being held at Makerere. It had been called at a critical time. "Winds of change" were sweeping Africa. Old certainties were under threat. So many new questions were being asked. The escalating violence against Christians in the Congo, with the rape and murder of nuns, was testing the moral codes of the clergy to the limit.

I was staying at Namilyango, fifteen miles from Kampala. It was the August holiday and the decision had been made that all residents at Makerere had to vacate their rooms. Priests, vicars, brothers and nuns were coming from every corner of Africa.

A huge agenda had been drawn up. A small sample of the paper titles on offer will give you an idea of the range of issues that was being discussed. I was particularly interested in the Jesuits' contributions. These were wide-ranging: 'The Challenge of the Evangelicals in Madagascar', 'Where is the Line Now in the War between Good and Evil?', 'Confronting Nudity in Karamoja', 'Is Cinema a Force for Good or Evil in the World of the 1960s?', 'James Bond, Good or Bad in the Modern World?, 'Attitudes to the Mini-Skirt in Contemporary African Society', 'Should the Wearing of the busuuti still be Encouraged?' The busuuti or gomesi is the traditional floor-length dress worn by women in Buganda.

The aim of the conference was to clear the air and establish new moral guidelines on these and a host of other pressing issues. I attached myself to the group of Spanish fathers and brothers, Jesuits from the Basque Country in northern Spain. I had always had a soft spot for them and had followed closely their attempt to create just societies in Latin America, specifically the Reductions of Paraguay.

I dropped in, out of personal interest, on the sessions on cinema. There was one where debate ranged between those who pointed out that the Bond films always upheld the triumph of good over evil and those who argued that such killing, on an industrial scale, in order to achieve a just end was contrary to Christian values and was never justified.

It so happened that the first Bond film, Dr No, was being shown again at the Odeon, now an ice cream factory. It starred Sean Connery as the fictional MI6 agent James Bond and Ursula Andress as Honey Ryder, a shell diver, who was making a living by selling Jamaican seashells to dealers in Miami.

Now, the manager of the Odeon was a friend of mine. He was an interesting character. He came from West Hampstead. He had taken to wearing Indian-style false beards and clothing. He ate nothing but curries. Theories abounded as to why he was doing this. These ranged from the idea that he was undergoing an identity crisis having grown up in a deprived working-class neighbourhood in London to the pecuniary, according to which he was trying to feather his nest by sucking up to wealthy Asian families in the city. A third hypothesis, Freudian, was that he had become fixated on the silk of saris. Even his speech had changed.

The decision was made at the conference that a working party would be set up to go and see the film. This was to be followed by an open discussion group. I tagged along.

As I have said, I admire the Jesuits. They seem to me to be very practical people. They value intellectual activity. Sometimes I question their policy of educating the elites in the countries they go to, but I have to acknowledge that they get results. Prior to the showing they asked me to introduce them to the manager, Tristram Applebaum. They wanted to examine the cinema's facilities, they said. They were duly shown round. I noticed that they were especially interested in the safety doors, even insisting on inspecting the tradesmen's entrance behind the stage. They nodded sagely to each other as they went round.

The film began. I sat between Father Izaguirre and Father Guevara from Loyola in the Basque Country. All was going well. The fathers were making notes, with some difficulty, in the dark. Cigarettes were being lit with more than customary frequency in order to facilitate note-taking. Suddenly there was a collective gasp. I looked up and saw a voluptuous woman emerging from the sea, dripping with water and wearing a white bikini. She appeared to be offering an erotic-looking conch shell.

The gasp was accompanied by a loud bang above us. The image of a growing burning hole appeared in the middle of the picture. Smoke could be seen billowing from the bright square through which the beam of the film was projected. The lights went on. My friend with the Indian beard appeared in front of us on the stage. He was wearing a white turban.

"Apologies to all of our patrons," he said, with an Indian accent, but will you all please vacate the premises immediately."

Panic broke out. People rushed to the exit at the back of the auditorium. The more they pushed, the more men and women became squashed in the doorway. Hardly anybody could get out.

Meanwhile, the fathers stood up calmly and, as if by clockwork and with military precision, moved in three separate and equal groups towards to the safety doors at the sides and the entrance behind the screen. They pushed the safety bars and emerged safely into the sunlight outside.

We all went on to the Uganda Bookshop for a coffee. This had been part of our original plan for the day. Father Ochoa led the discussion.

"Well, he began, this illustrates the wisdom of the world's first and greatest novelist, our very own Don Miguel de Cervantes Saavedra who in *El ingenioso hidalgo don Quijote de la Mancha*, Don Quixote of La Mancha, puts the following words into Sancho Panza's mouth: 'It is the part of a wise man to keep himself today for tomorrow, and not venture all his eggs in one basket.' Always keep your options open."

I lent forward and said. "I get it! You mean, do not put all your Basques in one exit!"
My words were met with a stony silence.

The Nightmare on Makindye Hill

Ken was a nervous young man. He was easily spooked. Some said he had a vivid imagination and that this magnified the fears that assailed him. He lived on Makindye Hill.

In bed in his nice Makindye house he had graphic dreams. They were so realistic that when they were happening he felt convinced that that he was really there.

One exceptionally lifelike dream came in the form of a nightmare. He would dream that he was running down Kampala Road pursued by a coffin. One feature of this bad dream was that if he went into a bank, a bar or a shop, the coffin would not follow him in. So in the dream this is what he would do. He would run up the steps into Barclays Bank, where he had an account, and would then feel safe. The good thing was that the coffin was not there when he left. However, it could appear from round a corner and start chasing him again, forcing him to dive in through the doors of National and Grindlay's bank or a bar like the Blue Flamingo.

In the dream he could be walking around any part of Kampala when it would happen. Some of his friends argued that he had dream anxiety disorder and that it had all started in 1966 when he was shot at at point-blank range when stopped by one of Amin's soldiers as he drove up towards the Kabaka's palace. Some call that day the Battle of Mengo. Ken had innocently got caught up in the events surrounding the expulsion by Obote of the Kabaka, the King. The bullet had just missed him. He had taken to wearing it as a memento on a necklace round his neck.

Be that as it may, he could not rid himself of the dream. He would be going to the loo at the back of the City Bar, for example, when, in the frame of the back door of the bar, the coffin would suddenly appear. His friends, in the dream, would be astonished to see him go flying out through the front door. These nocturnal visions were so convincing that he began to ask colleagues if they had witnessed the events depicted in them. His drinking pals were very understanding. Some put the dreams down to impurities in the poor beer that was served up in Kampala. Nile, Tusker, Club and Bell could leave one with a nasty hangover.

Things took a nasty term when he dreamt that he was going into a lecture. He worked in the faculty of Education. In his dream he had prepared a lengthy analysis of strikes in East African schools. He was going to examine twenty reasons why pupils struck. He had at last got to the bottom of it, he felt. The strikes were being fomented by local staff who were on far less money than expat teachers. You could say that the unrest was caused by envy, resentment, spite or a burning sense of injustice, depending on your political point of view, he was going to argue. In the dream he felt uneasy about this conclusion, as most of his students were Ugandan, but he felt obliged to say it. He was going into the lecture hall, which was full, when he heard a noise behind him. It was the coffin!

He ran down the steps inside the auditorium and up onto the stage from where he was supposed to give the lecture. The coffin followed him. He ran up the steps on the other side of the room and, pushing past the professor of Education, who had come to see what the fracas was about, rushed out of the building towards his car, followed by the coffin.

In terror - this was all part of the dream - he drove fast into Kampala. The coffin seemed to be catching up with him. There was only one thing for it. He had to get to Patel's, the Chemist's. He screeched to a halt outside the shop and ran in.

"What is the matter, Mr Cooke?" Mr Patel asked him. "Please sit down and catch your breath. Can I get you anything? A glass of water, a cup of tea?"

"You have to give me something, Mr Patel."

"But what for, Mr Cooke?"

"It's embarrassing to explain, Mr Patel," Ken Cooke said, throwing a nervous glance over his shoulder as he said it, "but you have to give me something to stop my coffin".

The Optometrist of Owino

Manubhai Patel was a small-time entrepreneur with huge ambition. He had several stalls in St Balikuddembe Market in Kampala, otherwise known as Owino Market.

He loved Owino. Each day as he opened his stall up, he would rub his hands together thinking of the 300,000 customers that would soon cram into it. At weekends even more would flow in. He felt a special bond with the 50,000 traders who operated there.

He had what he considered to be a brilliant idea. It was this. Thousands of his friends had been expelled from Uganda by Idi Amin in 1972. Many had opened very successful businesses in the UK. A cousin even had the contract for repairing furniture in the Houses of Parliament. Many of these businessmen and women were chemists, dentists and optometrists. He wrote to several hundred who had been personal friends of his before the exodus. He had escaped expulsion by taking out a Ugandan passport. It was a gamble but, well, that was the decision he had made. At times he regretted that he had not gone into exile with his friends but the upside was that he had spent most of his life amongst the familiar sounds, sights and smells of his childhood. He was in harmony with his surroundings. "Isn't that the definition of a happy man?" he would say to himself.

The letter he wrote to his friends in the United Kingdom read as follows:

"I am Manubhai. We were at school together in Kampala. I stayed here for reasons of which you will be aware. Life is good but money is short, very short. Please can you help me? All I ask is that you do the following.

If you are a dentist, please put a basket at Reception asking customers to donate their unwanted dentures to the Third World.

If you are a doctor or a chemist, please put a similar basket out for discarded and out-of-date medication.

If you are an optometrist, please ask customers to place their unwanted glasses in the basket."

The response Manubhai received was overwhelming, at least in the area of teeth and spectacles. Hundreds of sets of false teeth and pairs of glasses arrived at his house. He had to take on staff to sort them out and man his stalls. Eventually he was able to open up small lock-up shops with glass cases inside like the ones cousins of his had set up around the old Horse Hospital in Camden Lock Market in London.

There was always a crowd surrounding Manubhai's stalls. People queued up to try his teeth. He had mirrors hanging on secure chains from the ceilings of his little shops. Customers would pull strange faces as they tried to work out if the teeth they had selected would look good.

The same thing happened on the glasses stall. Gucci, Hugo Boss, Prada, Liberty London, Tiffany and Co., Oliver Peoples Gregory Peck - these could all be picked up for a song. His prices were very reasonable. After all, he had acquired them for nothing. Punters didn't worry that they couldn't see properly through them. It was the look, the 'Manubhai look', as it came to be known, that they were after.

Sunglasses became a very successful line, despite the fact that many were often terribly scratched and had loose hinges. Word would get round that Manubhai had a new stock of Dior, Chanel and Ray-Bans in. Junked Dior Reflecteds, Celine Shadows, Sunday Somewhere Laura Metals and Marc Jacobs Marcs became fashion statements on the streets of the capital.

Manubhai had other, future plans in Owino for cast-off, out-of-date clothing and abandoned shoes but for the time being he was content to concentrate on his present lines, particularly the thrown away glasses. These were proving to be his most lucrative source of income.

He had a letter from one of his brothers in Borehamwood. The supermarket in which the brother had a shop had suddenly torn up an agreement and asked him to vacate the premises by the end of the month. In a panic, Anil had written to Manubhai offering him his equipment. It was rather old-fashioned and, if truth be told, had been invented by Anil himself. It was cumbersome and heavy and would probably not have met the requirements of the Health and Safety inspectorate, had they been aware of its existence.

Manubhai was delighted to receive Anil's lens grinder, despite its ungainliness and excessive size. Its wheel was mounted horizontally on a stand borrowed from a tailor. It was operated with the same pedals that would have powered the sewing machine. Dust from grinding disappeared down a large hole in the middle. Manubhai went one better and had it linked to an erratic but powerful second hand motor that he had acquired from a colleague in the market.

His greatest pleasure consisted of grinding lenses. He would hum as the wheel hummed. His customers and fellow stall-holders loved to see him working away so happily. There was always a small crowd standing outside his shop looking in. They would comment on the lens grinder's obvious contentment.

One day he was grinding a particularly difficult lens when the motor suddenly went into top gear, so to speak. He was pulled forward and drawn towards the centre of the wheel. He tried to struggle free but his sleeve got caught up and his arm was sucked inexorably into the hole. In the struggle his turban unfurled and became caught up. Onlookers called out in alarm.

And that, dear readers, is the end of the story about the optometrist who fell into a lens grinder and made a spectacle of himself.

The Original African Shaggy Dog Story

Deogratias Olimba was trying to lead a peaceful life at Makerere. His wife Ruth had a dog she called Shaggy. Shaggy was, indeed, the shaggiest dog she had ever seen and she doted on him. He looked like a mop head on legs, except that you couldn't see his legs. Ruth sometimes called him "my Kentucky Multi-fold Mop".

The problem was keeping him clean in a hot climate. That was Deogratias's job. He had various techniques but the one that was least labour-intensive was to walk him down to the university swimming pool at night. He and Shaggy would squeeze through a gap in the hedge that students addicted to skinny-dipping had formed. Shaggy would swim up and down a few times and then together they would take a long walk back, popping into the Makerere staff bar en route.

Life proceeded calmly in the Olimba household. Ruth Olimba, an American, was very happy to pour her affection onto Shaggy. Deogratias was happy immersing himself in his research, contemporary African Politics. He was working on Pan-Africanism.

One day Shaggy went missing. Ruth was distraught. They sent out search parties of students to comb the city. Kampala was a very small place at that time. Nothing. There was no sign of Shaggy.

Ruth felt that the bottom had dropped out of her world. She began to nag Deogratias to do something. In fact, that is exactly what she kept screaming, "Do something!" Deogratias realised that his life would not be worth living unless he found the dog.

Now, Deogratias's problem was that he did not like dogs. He had come to terms with his wife's pet because it kept her happy and off his back. She could have a sharp, shrill tongue.

To say that he did not like dogs is an understatement. He was, deep down, a cynophobe. He knew this but it didn't become obvious to him until he launched his plan to retrieve Shaggy. He came to the conclusion that Ruth's pet had joined the pack of semi-feral dogs that roamed the campus at night.

What had happened was this. Makerere was staffed mainly by ex-pats. At the end of two or three year contracts, lecturers and their families would pack up and head off back home to the UK and the USA. Many had acquired dogs. There were just too many to be absorbed by new, incoming staff and, anyway, the expat cohort was shrinking year by year as posts became Africanised. The abandoned pets formed a band of brothers and sisters that raided the rubbish bins on the campus at night. They moved at great speed. They always seemed to be running and, frankly, they terrified Deogratias.

Nevertheless, he had to get Shaggy back, or a dog like Shaggy, in order to restore some semblance of normality in his marriage. He began to patrol the university grounds with a butterfly net. He hid behind bushes and waited for the pack of dogs to run by. He had some strips of raw steak in a carrier taken from his fridge.

Sure enough, the dogs appeared, barking and howling as they went by. There was a shaggy dog amongst them. It wasn't Shaggy but, Deogratias thought, perhaps he could be a substitute. Suddenly the dogs stopped running. They sniffed the air and turned their heads towards the bush where Deo - Ruth called him that - was hiding. A low collective growl could be heard and, in the dim light, bared teeth could be seen. Deogratias started to run. He ran as fast as he could back towards the block of flats where he and Ruth lived. He managed to outrun the dogs and he slammed the door behind him just as they were about to sink their teeth into him.

"Deo, why did you slam the door like that?" his wife called down ear-splittingly.

"It's nothing, dear. Just the wind," he called back.

The following night he adopted a different plan. He had a word with one of the security men on campus. They drove Mini Mokes around the grounds. He borrowed one. He drove slowly along the straight roads, the net sticking out of the side. The Moke that he had chosen had a canvas hood and plastic windows so he felt reasonably safe. Then he saw the pack again. They seemed to be engaged in a play fight of sorts.

He drove up to them and dangled a piece of steak out of the window just as he passed the white shaggy dog he had seen the night before. Under the street light he realised that that many of the dogs could be described as shaggy. Several had long, thick, unkempt hair. Perhaps if it he could just net one of those, it would do the trick with Ruth. He couldn't take his eyes off the white one, though.

As if by a miracle, the white shaggy dog returned his stare and came running towards the piece of steak. Right at the last moment Deogratias pulled his arm in and the dog leapt into the vehicle in pursuit of a juicy meal.

Then the rest of the pack realised what was happening and came running towards the car. Deo was panic-stricken. With his heart in his mouth and shaking like a leaf, he accelerated away from the vicious, hungry pack. Round and round the campus he drove trying to put a distance between himself and the bared fangs. "Is this how it is going to end?" he muttered, as he pressed the pedal into the floor.

To his relief, he saw another Mini Moke approaching. It was the askaris, the nighwatchmen. They leapt out, waved their arms and shouted something at the dogs that simply turned and ran.

Deo's heart was still beating fast as he went up the stairs of his flat with the replacement shaggy dog in his arms.

"Ruth, look what I have got for you," he gasped.

"I am sorry, Deo," she screeched, "but that dog is just not shaggy enough! Get rid of it immediately! He has to go!"

The Terrifyingly High Pier of Port Bell

He was a nice chap. We called him "Clint". That was irony. His real name was Dave. He was a mild-mannered man. He was in my MA in Comparative African Literature class at Makerere. I was specialising in the poetry of the Spanish and Portuguese-speaking countries of Africa. Eventually both he and I got good jobs lecturing in African Literature, he in the States, I in London. Time and places change people. I almost went to Orange County but they were running out of young men for Vietnam. He went to Connecticut. We got back in touch recently.

I remember his landlady, Mrs Fisher. She was a smiley lady who was always sitting down. Her skin looked glaucous. It had a shiny, not dull, greyish-blue colour. "She loves her gin", I was told.

Dave shared the flat with Miles. Miles was not his real name. That was Brian. Brian had become Miles at school, through a strange process of alchemy then in vogue. They were both Londoners but seemed as different as chalk from cheese. I was more friendly with Miles than with Dave. Dave was more reserved. Miles was out-going.

I remember the flat that Dave and Miles rented from Mrs Fisher. It was not far from the back door of the City Bar. She was one of the few Europeans who rented out flats. It was old and damp. I remember a big barrel of beer in the middle of the veranda floor put there for a party. The floor bowed and looked as if it was about to cave in. Looking back, Kampala was a great place. I know I benefited hugely from it.

I knew Miles better than Dave. Miles, as we always called him, used to rag Dave. He, we, as I have said, called Dave "Clint", after Clint Eastwood, I suppose. He wasn't like Clint Eastwood at all.

(Dave tells me now that he was called Crint, not Clint, after a very camp and effeminate man played by Peter Sellers in 'The Goon Show', a type of official, one Jim Crint Flowerdew. I do not remember Clint or Crint as being effeminate. It was all part of the ribbing.)

Be that as it may, Miles implied that Dave was softer than he was. Miles could be competitive but I suspect that Dave gave him as good as he got. He didn't do it in public though. I felt Miles was slightly cruel to Dave. Dave suffered in silence when Miles pulled his leg in front of others. Miles used to do it to me, perhaps, but I ignored it, which he liked. My ego was a little bit stronger than Dave's was then. I was also slightly older. I can't remember if Dave had been to public school. I imagined then that, like me, he hadn't. Miles had strong self-belief. I think this, curiously, was good for Dave. It made Dave say to himself that he was all right too. Miles didn't do it so much, the putting down, with me. I felt that Dave was possibly hiding his light under a bushel. He was a bit shy and was wary of The City Bar, although I think he liked a half with me and Danny and others in the humbler pub, the International Bar, at the foot of Kololo Hill near where our tutor, Dr Aurora Chaleco, from Trinidad, lived. Dr Chaleco and I exchanged emails not so long ago. She's in Cuba now.

I am trying to remember Dave's girlfriend's name. I have a feeling he had a girl in London. Her skin didn't look too good. She wore heavy make-up. Yes, she came out to Uganda to visit. This clipped Dave's wings a little.

Miles used to say "Naff off, Clint", or something stronger, to Dave all the time. Dave would smile. It was all a bit Top Gear-ish, Jeremy Clarkson versus James May. I felt Dave was wary about being perceived as "one of the lads". I have a feeling respectability mattered to him. I could go on for ages about that.

I remember snatches of conversation:

Me: "We are off for a pint! Coming?"
Dave: "Er, I have that essay to finish for Agnes" [Dr Agnes Shefford].
Me: "Oh stop being a goody-goody! Blow Agnes! Come on, Clint!"
Dave: "Tomorrow."

To be honest, I didn't like the way Miles treated Dave. I often felt like telling Miles but I didn't, concluding that it was none of my business. He was always going about "blooming Simpson". He may have said, "What a drag he is. Can't get him to do anything" - that sort of thing. It was a strange relationship. I often asked myself why Dave put up with it. I concluded that he and Miles wanted a flat in the city centre, away from the campus, and could only afford it by pooling their resources.

Miles was into glamour - Hilary Highgate. In later years she and he would visit me and my wife in our flat back in north London. She would collapse on the sofa and ask for a cup of tea, gasping "My back!" High maintenance. No, that's not fair, she did have a bad back. Miles seemed hen-pecked. He was always rushing about on some errand or other to please her. I have a feeling he was vulnerable. As you know, Dr Ferdinand, the Comparative Literature Professor, loved him because he was working-class and had been a scholarship boy at a leading London public school. The social experiment had been a success in Dr Ferdinand's eyes. She, Dr Aurita Ferdinand, from Río Muni, Equatorial Guinea, was left-wing. Her family had strong upper-class ties with England but that's another story. I have a feeling it had stressed Miles out going to that school. It did his health in in the end. Dave was "all at sea", I suspect, about what was going on, inside Miles's head. Discretion was the greater part of valour, for Dave. Miles went on to do stocks and shares as a side-line, which I think was very bad for him, for his nerves. I had a suspicion Miles needed Dave to boost his ego. I guess Dave was a bit bemused by this. I suppose Miles had the public school boy's need to feel, and be seen to be, top dog. But he didn't do it with me. A job came up in Mozambique. I told Miles I was applying. I felt I had a strong case. He hadn't heard about it. He applied without telling me and was called for interview. I felt miffed about that and our friendship cooled a little thereafter.

I dread to think what Dave thought about me. At that time I couldn't have cared less what people thought. I was into carpe diem, grabbing hungrily at each second. I think it annoyed our African Linguistics lecturer, Agnes, that I was so unconcerned about what she thought. She concluded, "not public school material", I am sure. I was never invited on her Makerere Madrigal Choir tours of Lourenço Marques, or Maputo, as it is now called. Mind you, I couldn't sing. You should have seen Agnes's face when I walked in for the interview for the Chair in Accra, or was it Abuja? She said, with a self-satisfied, false-sincere expression, "Sorry. Wheels within wheels, you know." She and I clashed over Annie. There was talk of careers in MI5 or MI6 and even the Ugandan Secret Service - there were so few modern languages graduates specialising in Africa then. I was totally turned off by the idea.

Agnes offered me 'Thieves Slang in Luanda' and 'The Influence of North Africa in The Gypsy Language of Andalusia' as possible PhD topics. She was trying to get rid of me, I concluded.

I have a feeling Dave felt that it was necessary to keep his head down, not to blot his copy-book, which was all too easy in small town Kampala, as it was then, where nearly everyone knew where and with whom nearly everyone else was sleeping. I have a feeling Dave felt that he had possibly stuck his neck out too far by moving into a trendy flat. I was envious. It was cool. It made Dave careful about what he did and said. He worried, I suspect, that people might report anything negative he might have said. I can hardly remember Dave saying anything now. This was very sensible, I felt. Anyway, it is very English to be self-effacing. God knows how Dave managed to cope with in-your-face, *"my son's going to be the next president"* America. In Africa and the UK we knew that there was not much on offer and that there was no need to strut one's stuff on the stage of life. It would not lead anywhere unless you were born into the right circles. There was Percy, the Right Honourable Percy Chiswick, whose area of expertise was the Literatures of Anglophone Africa. He became the UK's man in the Middle East. Blithering idiot. And Agnes! Well! I have just written a novel in which some of this comes up.

    I was fascinated by Miles because of his combination of working class lad and upper middle class schoolboy. I don't think he was at ease with the in-set on Nakasero. Strangely, I fitted in with the "nobs". Times were a-changing. All that class stuff was beginning to crumble. I have a feeling Dave was nervous about moving into the new areas that were opening up. He clung to his childhood sweetheart: "And always keep a-hold of nurse, for fear of finding something worse". I found them, the posh set, fascinating. What they were doing in Kampala, I don't know. Many had ties with Kenyan settlers. There were the renegade daughters of conservative London entrepreneurs, like Mary of the famous British newspaper family. It was the world of A level English novels, in pockets. I tumbled into them. Don't ask me how it happened but I had a classy accent. Miles did too, to some extent, but you could hear the Cockney underneath, both in his intonation and the structures. Hilary adopted a Mockney manner, a rough way of speaking, as if trying to hide her middle class origins. Miles was not into playing the field. Hilary didn't know what to make of me really.

    Miles had a mixture of working-class aggressiveness - if you are at the bottom of the pile you have to have it - plus a public school bossiness and assertiveness. If you are on top you have to fight to preserve your power. Call it self-confidence, if you like, or arrogance. Miles had to be right (almost) all the time. That's what they teach you. Dave and I were, I suspect, lower-middle class, at least for a while. I liked to boast that I was working class but I am sure I was not a very convincing specimen in my jeans, Harris tweed jacket and suede shoes. We tended to keep our heads down and work hard, rarely venturing to raise them above the parapet. I did that a bit more than Dave, perhaps, when I parodied Dr Ferdinand, the Prof, using her phrases, "it seems to me" and so on, at the away day conference centre that the university owned in the mountains of Kigezi. Kigezi coffee! I still remember it. God knows how I got away with the parodying. I probably didn't. I could be wrong, by the way, about Dave's social class then. I must ask him.

I often felt Dave didn't look well. Miles and I would go off jogging each day. He was glowing with health. I was too. He would often comment that Dave would not venture out into the fresh air, into the sun. He did look pale, did Dave. I put it down to bad food. I concluded that he and Miles were spending too much of their money on the rent. Perhaps Hilary - she was wealthy - cooked Miles some fillet steak, some filet mignon, in her digs.

One day Miles and I decided that Dave needed to get out more. A rich student called Kenneth Sinclair-Otieno kept a rather spectacular rowing boat in a lock-up down by the jetty in Port Bell, where the flying boats used to land. He called it a Thames wherry. It was in fact built to an eighteenth century design. It needed more than one person to get it going. We persuaded Ken to lend it to us. Our friend Dave needed to exercise and breathe in some good lake air, we argued. He needed to get out of his gloomy flat. Ken consented.

After considerable arm-twisting, Dave agreed to come rowing with us. The lake was choppy and we pushed the boat on its trolley to the end of the jetty. As we went past the plaque that said 'Port Bell Pier 3730 feet', I saw a look of alarm spread across Dave's face. His jaw dropped and he went white. His head began to spin and his eyes glazed over. He felt he was going to faint.

"Right, Dave, this is the moment of truth. You launch the boat," Miles said.

Dave peered over the edge. He pulled back.

"I can't do it!" he cried, "I just can't".

"Why on earth not?" Miles barked angrily.

Dave replied with a sheepish grin: "It's a long way to tip a wherry!"

The Sad Tale of Rwenzori Rory

Alex Munro was an intrepid explorer. At least he liked to think he was. He even wore pith helmets, of which he had two, one white, the other a puce colour. He liked to wear a bush jacket made of lightweight, tan cotton twill with bellows, a belt and pleated pockets for more storage space. Four symmetrical, flapped front pockets and epaulettes gave him a paramilitary look. He liked that. When he stepped out of his Land Rover in the Ugandan bush, he felt like Clark Gable in the film *Mogambo*. He was proud of his safari boots and the white socks that came up to the knee, almost touching the bottom of his camouflaged shorts.

There were not many places left to explore in Africa. Alex spent much time trying to identify where they were. He had been reduced, eventually, to retracing the tracks of famous explorers, like Stanley, Livingstone, Burton, Speke and Teleki.

Running out of ideas in that field, he began to search Africa for unusual animals: civets, aardvarks, galagos, elephant shrews, gerenuks and the like. Neighbours on the Makerere campus began to complain about the strange noises coming from pens in his back garden.

Now, Nature can produce very unusual creatures. Alex began to home in on them, travelling to Madagascar for both the Aye-Aye and the Lowland Streaked Tenrec. He sought out the pink, pig-like Hippopotamus by a river in Kenya. He even went further afield, to the Galapagos for the Red-Lipped Batfish. His neighbours at Makerere began to complain even more. It had no effect on Alex. His collecting was becoming an obsession. He began to seek out freaks of Nature.

One day, a chap who worked in a Ugandan game park knocked on his door. He had a large box with him.

"I think I may have found what you are looking for, Mr Munro," the park ranger whispered. He opened the box.

"What is it?" asked Alex.

"We don't know. It's an oddity, a mutant perhaps. It was found in the mountains to the west."

Alex had heard rumours of a privately funded genetic engineering institute somewhere near The Mountains of the Moon, the Rwenzoris, but so far had come across no proof of its existence.

Esau, the ranger, lifted the creature out of the box. At first Alex thought it might be some sort of African Pygmy Hedgehog. He could see its eyes twinkling. But no, this animal was too big to be that. He had never seen anything like it in his life. To all intents and purposes, it consisted of a large furry head. The other parts of its body were either hidden in the fur or were totally undeveloped.

Alex fell in love with it. Initially, he called it, simply, "Head". He could think of no other way of categorising it. He became more and more fond of it, even to the point of taking it out with him when he went into Kampala. He and Head became inseparable. He doted on Head and Head doted on him.

Weeks, months, almost a year went by and Head continued to grow bigger and bigger. Alex decided to try him out in a testing adult situation. He took him to the City Bar.

He walked in, carrying Head in his arms. He toyed with the idea of christening him there and then as "Rory": Rory Head. He had had a good friend at school with that name. Neighbours were calling Head Rwenzori Rory, after the area where he had been found.

He put his companion on a stool at the bar. Babu didn't blink an eyelid. He was used to eccentric Europeans and, anyway, he had had a soft spot for Alex ever since he heard that the Scotsman's wife had left him to go back to Sweden. Babu had been having similar problems in his family. A cousin's wife had just packed her bags and gone back to Gujarat.

"He's just a head, Babu," Alex said.

Babu nodded.

"Two pints, please. One for me and one for Head."

"Coming up," Babu shouted from his stool in his usual corner behind the bar.

Rory stuck his tongue into his glass and started sucking. Soon he had almost drained the glass of its contents. Suddenly an arm shot out on the right hand side under his head. A hand grasped the glass and poured the remaining liquid down his throat. He banged the glass down, clearly signalling that he wanted another.

At first, Alex hesitated. He whispered "I think you should quit now, Rory Head". Rory was having none of it. "Oh, well, why not?" Alex thought, taken aback by the appearance of the arm. Curiously, though, he was not entirely surprised, as if he suspected all along that this might happen.

Another glass of Tusker was downed and then another arm appeared. Rory was beginning to resemble a recognisable mammal, a bear-like animal, a throw-back, perhaps, to the now extinct African Atlas Bear, perhaps. But had that got down as far south as the mountains of Uganda in the past and with what had it mated? Had that lost Roman legion brought it with them as a mascot?

Rory banged the empty glass down again. A leg appeared. Another beer produced the other leg. He was now whole and people were peering at him to try and identify the species he belonged to.

Suddenly, he jumped off his stool, ran down the steps into the busy Kampala Road and was run over by a passing car.

Alex was inconsolable. He began wailing as Rory's lifeless body was carried into the bar.

"I blame myself, Babu," he cried, "and I also blame my lost friend, Rory Head. He wouldn't stop. It was too much for him."

"Don't blame yourself, Alex," Babu said. I heard you tell him he should have quit while he was a head."

The Talking Dog of Kisenyi

Wesley Barrow was an academic. He was doing a PhD on 'Talking Animal Myths' in the Department of Anthropology at Makerere University College, Kampala. His thesis plan fell into the following chapters: Birds, Dogs, Elephants, Goats, Cats, Harbour Seals, Beluga Whales, Mongooses, Chickens and Cryptids.

His secret desire was to encounter a talking cryptid. He had a hidden library of books on them: the Jersey Devil, the South African Grootslang, or Great Snake, the Irish Dobhar-Chú, or Water Hound, the Akkorokamui (a giant Japanese octopus), the Bolivia/Brazil borderland Mapinguari and Luton's Black Shuck. Wesley hailed from Luton in Bedfordshire, a county that lies to the north of London. Some colleagues were slightly worried about him. His secret library was a subject of gossip in the Makerere staff bar and people worried that Welsey's judgement, his scientific objectivity, might have become befuddled. There was even a rumour emerging that the only qualification he had was an HND in Hotel and Catering from Hendon College of Technology in North London.

He had just delivered a paper at a symposium held at the Game Lodge in Murchison Falls National Park on 'Superstitions Surrounding Talking Chickens with Reference to Fears about the Future'. There was some nervousness in the Department as Wesley had referred to a chicken that was alleged to have spoken to the Dictator, foretelling his imminent demise. The gentleman in question had taken to sleeping in a different house every night. The Dean had told Wesley that he would not be able to protect him if there were any repercussions as a result of the paper.

Be that as it may, Wesley was a brave soul and refused to be cowed. He carried on driving around Kampala in his blue Ford Zephyr 4. The car was the pride of his life.

He was driving through Kisenyi, essentially a slum area in the middle of Kampala, when he saw a sign in front of a shack: "Talking Dog for Sale".

He screeched to a halt, sending up a cloud of orange dust. He knocked on the door. The owner called out "Go round the back".

Wesley went into back yard and saw the dog, a large black German Shepherd with yellow eyes, tied a post. The creature reminded him of drawings he had seen in books of Black Shuck.

"Can you speak?" he asked the dog.

"Pardon?" the dog replied.

"Do you talk?"

"Yes," barked the dog.

"Do tell me your story", Wesley said.

"I found out that I could talk when I was not much more than a puppy. I felt that I could, perhaps, be useful to my country so I went to the main police station in the centre of Kampala and told them about my talent.

To cut a long story short, they took me on as an informer, or spy, if you like. I would wander into the Russian Embassy and would eavesdrop conversations about which politicians, ministers and academics were in the pay of the KGB. I would then trot across to the American Embassy to listen in at meetings between CIA agents and local dignitaries. I attended the key meeting in which it came out that the CIA was funding a magazine for intellectuals called *Transformation*. I was given a month's supply of juicy eland bones for that piece of information. The Prime Minister, who felt that he was staying on top of things as my snippets poured in, had a special medal cast for me for me to hang on my collar."

"Can I see it?" asked Wesley.

"Sadly I lost it when I was running away from a furious soldier in the local military barracks. He had seen me watching him unload a lorry filled with gold bars with the words "Gouvernement du Congo" stamped on them. He actually fired at me and the medal got caught as I clambered over the wire fence."

"I see," said Wesley.

"That incident gave me a shock. I decided that I needed to change my life-style. I asked if I could be assigned to Security at Entebbe Airport. This was agreed and I settled down to a regular routine of uncovering smugglers, criminals and terrorists. I took to sniffing them out whilst staying silent.

Again I was awarded many honours, many medals, which I keep inside Mr Mukasa's shack. I have settled down now, retired. I am married and have many puppies."

Wesley Barrow was by now dumbfounded. The incident had thrown him completely. He had always been able to explain phenomena like talking parrots but this was something else. He turned towards Mukasa's hut.

"How much do you want for the dog?" he shouted through the glassless window.

"Oh, not much, shillingi ishirini, twenty shillings?"

"Twenty shillings for a dog with such a gift? How come?"

"Oh, he is such a liar. He didn't do any of those things!"

The Tin Man of Nakasero

Makerere University's Academic Board held a meeting in the white-fronted, blue window-framed Main Building. It was decided that they had to be seen to be embracing the twentieth century. Oil had been discovered in breath-taking quantities in various parts of the country. There was money for some eye-catching projects.

A Department of Robotics and Cyborg Technology was set up. The idea was sold to the army on the grounds that Uganda's porous borders needed to be controlled effectively and in such a way that would cut down on the number of casualties suffered by incursions from the LRA, the Lord's Resistance Army, in the north and from rebel Congolese and Rwandese attacks in the west.

One of the new department's first projects was Robotic and Cyborg Warfare. Intelligent, machine-gun and rocket-bearing drones had already been purchased abroad and were creating a successful no man's land in areas used in the past by terrorists of various hues.

The idea of a "human weapon" had been gleaned from Hollywood films that were popular in Kampala at the time, like *Cyborg Soldier* and *Iron Man*. The Ministry of Defence had given its blessing to the project and had promised its full cooperation. Benjamin Kisosonkole and Simon Chekamundo were put in charge.

Work started in a secret laboratory built under one of the pyramid-shaped hills that characterise the landscape of the capital city. A system of underground tunnels was constructed rapidly with tunneling machines flown in, broken up and boxed, from Stansted Airport near London. The boring machines Jessica and Ellie were brought in once the Pudding Mill Lane to

Stepney Green part of the Underground Crossrail project had been completed. They were joined by Phyllis and Ada when the Royal Oak to Farringdon line was completed.

Benjamin's pet project was the Cyborg Soldier. He himself volunteered to be the guinea pig. Work began in earnest in the depths of Nakasero Hill. This was a prime, strategic location. Not only was it near government offices in the city but special lifts to laboratories could be constructed under ministers' houses dotted around the circumference of the hill. It had symbolic importance too. In the history of Uganda it had been associated with warfare since the building of Lugard's Fort on its summit.

Experiments began seeking to "weld" various metals to Ben's skin. There was ample wolfram in the country but tungsten, that comes from it, is difficult to bend. As a purely preliminary first stage, it was decided that Ben would be coated with tin. The DR Congo had mountains of the stuff and it was readily available from there at a knock-down price.

The work progressed well and Ben began to feel quite at home in his new covering. Unwisely, perhaps, the powers-that-be decided to show Ben off. He was taken to parties and other official events held in the American, British, French and Chinese embassies. Ben, now openly called The Tin Man, even walked the cat-walk with star male and female models at a fashion event organised by the French in the Kampala Serena Hotel. Ambassadors' wives exchanged selfies of themselves with their arms around - and even kissing - The Tin Man. Shops in Kampala began to stock Tin Man suits and dresses. The fashion spread like wild-fire to Nairobi and Dar es Salaam. It is rumoured that a famous economist who lectures at a prestige university in Tanzania even wears a tin suit he bought in David Saddler, the upmarket men's clothing store in Dar, when he is giving lectures on 'The Future of Metals in East and Central Africa'.

All this fame was going to Ben's head. Putting up with the itching and the discomfort that having a tin skin was causing him, he began to parade around the city in an open-topped car, an old and rather tinny-looking MG of the sort that Spitfire pilots drove in Battle of Britain films. Ben was becoming a celebrity.

Whispers were heard that he was harbouring political ambitions. There was even one that he had his eyes on the Presidency. Elections were due later that year. He had not denied that he might be a candidate. Secretly, in fact, he was drawing up campaign plans and had been putting together not only an election team but a future cabinet.

News of this reached certain ears in the country. Someone in the Ministry of Works and Transport got wind of The Tin Man's ambitions. Meetings took place in dark corners of bars in the Speke Hotel, the Hotel Africana and the Uganda Golf Club. Phone calls were made to the British and American Military attachés offices. A plot was hatched in the Kampala Club.

Ben was going to give a speech to Tin Man followers in the beautiful Sheraton Gardens in the centre of Kampala. It was advertised as a family event. Parents were asked to bring their children. Presents would be handed out, it was announced. Children knew what that meant. Tin Man figures were selling like hot cakes throughout East Africa and beyond. They were outperforming Luke Skywalker and Princess Leia effigies. Ben had ordered boxes of new ones with different features, laser guns and missile shields, for example. Excitement was mounting.

Ben was helped up onto a makeshift, wooden platform near the Sheraton Hotel. His team began to unload boxes of figurines from the back seat of his MG. The atmosphere was electric. Ben approached the microphone to begin his speech. He was about to announce that he was standing for president.

An almighty din arose behind him. He couldn't turn round quickly, as his technicians had not yet perfected the necessary mechanisms for such a movement. The ground seemed to be shaking and windows in the hotel were rattling. He couldn't see what was coming but the crowd could. All he could hear was a loud chugging, like that of a train struggling to get up the side of the Rift Valley in Kenya, as an old-fashioned British-era steam-roller, an Aveling and Porter, came lumbering down the incline behind him and towards the very podium on which he was standing. He just managed to move his feet sufficiently to face the mechanical monster just before it struck.

The crowd was horrified. Dreams of a new future, of a "new Uganda" to be forged in the "white heat" of a "scientific revolution" - Ben had drawn heavily on Harold Wilson's speeches - lay crushed, nay completely flattened, on the grass. The steam roller sped on down the hill. Followers formed a protective circle around their dying leader in case souvenir-hunting children grabbed pieces of the special, almost holy, metal. They all leant forward to see if they could make out his dying words. They could just hear the following, whispered from crushed lips: "I have been foiled!"

Notes

These notes on aspects of popular culture are intended mainly as an aid for students learning English as a foreign language. The puns upon which these stories depend often require a certain amount of 'ingroup' knowledge.

The Bell-Ringer of Monmartre

'**Singin' In the Rain**', a song with lyrics by **Arthur Freed** and music by **Nacio Herb Brown, first appeared** in 1929. The film with that title came out in 1952. Some critics call it the best movie musical.

The Bowling Green Man of Entebbe

'**For whom exactly the Tells bowled.**' *For Whom the Bell Tolls*, a novel by **Ernest Hemingway**, was published in 1940. It is set in the Spanish Civil War of 1936-1939. Hemingway was inspired by a poem written by the metaphysical poet John Donne published in 1624 in a book of meditations titled *Devotions upon Emergent Occasions* (Meditation XVII).

"No man is an *Iland*, intire of it selfe; every man is a peece of the *Continent*, a part of the *maine*; if a *Clod* bee washed away by the *Sea*, *Europe* is the lesse, as well as if a *Promontorie* were, as well as if a *Mannor* of thy *friends* or of *thine owne* were; any mans *death* diminishes *me*, because I am involved in *Mankinde*; And therefore never send to know for whom the *bell* tolls; It tolls for *thee*."

[Modern English: No man is an island, entire of itself; every man is a piece of the continent, a part of the main. If a clod be washed away by the sea, Europe is the less, as well as if a promontory were, as well as if a manor of thy friend's or of thine own were: any man's death diminishes me, because I am involved in mankind, and therefore never send to know for whom the bells tolls; it tolls for thee.]

The Dead Ringer

'His face rang a bell'. The normal expression is "His (or her) face rings a bell". A possible origin of this saying lies in the fairground attraction consisting of a metal plate or large "button" that you hit with a large wooden mallet in an effort to send a small weight up a slide to ring a bell at the top of a tall post or board. In boxing, a "bell ringer" refers to the knock-out blow, the point at which a bell is rung to signal the end of a fight. Compare the modern expression "a light-bulb moment" to indicate sudden illumination.

The Englishman Called Hugh

'Only Hugh can prevent florist friars'. "Only YOU Can Prevent Forest Fires" comes from America and involves Smokey the Bear, an advertising **mascot** created to inform the public about the dangers of forest fires. Smokey Bear's slogan, "Remember... Only YOU Can Prevent Forest Fires" was created in 1947 by the US **Advertising Council.** Nearly all adults in America will recognise it.

The Fiendish Uganda Bookshop Plot

'Don't put all your exes into one basket!' 'To put all one's eggs in one basket' may go back to 1710 when Samuel Palmer, in his M*oral Essays on some of The most Curious and Significant English, Scotch and Foreign Proverbs*, London, wrote "Don't venture all your eggs in one basket". However, Sancho Panza in Don Quixote (Part I, Book III, Chapter 9) by Miguel de Cervantes [1547-1616] said: "It is the part of a wise man to keep himself today for tomorrow, and not venture all his eggs in one basket." (Incidentally, the punning expression "to put all one's Basques in one exit", may have originated in 1939.) One might hear it said in the City of London with the meaning, "Spread your risks or investments so that if one enterprise fails you will not lose everything." Martin H. Manser in *The Facts on File Dictionary of Proverbs* writes: "The proverb was first recorded in English in the 17th century in Giovanni Torriano's *A Common Place of Italian Proverbs and Proverbial Phrases*, and is probably of Spanish or Italian origin. He argues that there was an earlier English proverb "Venture not all in one bottom [of a ship]", of Latin origin.

The Gigantic Soroti Coffin

'**Everybody knows that cough drops stop coughin**'.' At the end of this story there is parody of the song 'Money is the root of all evil'. It is the tune that is copied here. This saying, about money and evil, derives from the Bible: the 'First Epistle to Timothy' in the New Testament (1 Timothy 6:10, KJV): "For the love of money is the root of all kinds of evil." There is a Latin proverb: Radix malorum est cupiditas, "Greed is the root of all evil". The film *Money is the Root of all Evil* came out in 1946. In the UK, in the 1940s, 50s and 60s, the song was on almost everybody's lips. You could not escape it. One of the Andrews Sisters' versions of the song is available on YouTube.

Coughin' / coffin. There are several versions of a shaggy dog story involving a play on the words coughing (coughin') and coffin. Some resemble variations on the stories of phantom funerals.

There is a punning 'poem' that is often heard in the UK:

*It's not the cough
that carries you off,
It's the coffin
they carry you off in.*

This is said to be a skipping song. In Victorian times, before penicillin, a cough could often mean you would be dead within a fortnight. It could be viewed as a death jibe, a taunting of death.

It is common in speech to drop the final 'g' in words that end in the letters 'ing' and the initial 'h'. In Luton, where I grew up, we used to say about a rival town, Hitchin:

Go to 'itchin
Come back scratchin'.

The Girl with the Glass Eye

'Only if they catch my eye.' To catch someone's eye', meaning to be attractive to the person looking, as well as to catch or get someone's attention, is a curious expression. He caught my eye = I found him attractive. It is difficult to find an exact equivalent in other languages. French: Attirer (to draw, to attract) l'attention de quelqu'un, Spanish: Llamar (to call) la atención de alguien, Swahili: kupata mawazo ya mtu (kupata, to get, mawazo, a thought, an idea, mtu, person).

The Hills of Uganda

'**The Hills are alive with the sound of music**' is a line from the title song of the 1959 musical *The Sound of Music*, music composed by **Richard Rodgers**, lyrics by **Oscar Hammerstein II**. First sung by Mary Martin in the original 1959 Broadway production, its best known version is by Julie Andrews in the musical drama film *The Sound of Music* (1965) about the von Trapp family escaping from the Nazis.

The Kampalan Clairvoyant

'**I Can See Clearly Now**', a song written and recorded by **Johnny Nash**, was a single from the album of the same name. It achieved success in the USA and the UK when it was released in 1972. John Lester "Johnny" Nash, Jr. was born on August 19, 1940 in Houston, Texas. He is an **American reggae singer-songwriter**, best known in America for this very **hit in 1972**, '**I Can See Clearly Now**'. He was one of the first non-Jamaican singers to record reggae music in **Kingston, Jamaica**.

The Lord of Nyamuliro

'**People who live in glass houses shouldn't throw stones.**' This saying means: Do not criticize others for bad qualities that you have yourself, do not criticise others if you have similar weaknesses. In the story Patrick criticises people in power in Kampala for their foibles but then his world falls apart at the hands of their agents. It can also mean that you shouldn't start a fight when you are vulnerable. It is about hypocrisy and vulnerability. Vulnerable people should not attack others.

The Optometrist of Owino

'**To make a spectacle of oneself**', an expression that may come from America, means to embarrass oneself or others in public, to draw attention to oneself in a ridiculous way, to do something that makes you look stupid. 'Spectacle' came into English from the Latin spectaculum, a show, a spectacle, via the French spectacle. Consider the word 'spectacular' - a spectacular victory, defeat. The Latin verb spectare means 'to watch'. 'To spectate' exists as a verb meaning 'to be present as a spectator' but it does not feel quite right yet in British English. The first example of the word spectacles (glasses) in the sense of glass lenses comes from circa 1430, according to the Oxford English Dictionary. The pun in this story exploits the two meanings of the word 'spectacle'. Note that it is essentially wrong to say 'a spectacle' for one of the lenses of a pair of spectacles. To extract the humour, the story sins against the norms of grammar.

The Sad Tale of Rwenzori Rory

'**To quit while one is ahead**', meaning 'to quit before one begins to lose', is heard in motor racing circles, in casinos, card games and in the Stock Exchange. 'Don't push your luck' has a similar meaning.

The Music Man of Kololo

'**I saw her face**' is a phrase taken from the song 'I'm a Believer' composed by **Neil Diamond** and recorded by the pop group **The Monkees** in 1966. The line of the song that most people knew by heart in the nineteen-sixties was:
Then I saw her face, now I'm a believer.

'It's a Long Way to Tipperary' has a strong presence in British popular culture. It was sung by soldiers in France during the First World War. It is in many ways the song of that war. It started life as a music hall song and may have been the result of a five shilling bet made in Stalybridge on 30 January, 1912. It was written by Jack Judge and co-credited to Harry Williams (Henry James Williams).

Soldiers sang it as they marched along briskly. It is a marching song sung to lift the spirits on confronting almost certain death at the front. It was brought back from the trenches in 1918-19. It was part of many a collection of bakelite records in the 1920s, 30s, 40s and 50s. People still sing it when they are together, e.g. on coach trips to the sea, in pubs as a drinking song and in general social sing-alongs.

Tipperary is in Ireland. Many Irish soldiers fought in that war. Ireland was part of Britain then. Signs in the county of Tipperary humorously declare: "You've come a long, long way …". Jack Judge came from Ireland. Many Irish men and women came to England at that time. There is a song from 1909 called 'Long Way to Connemara'. Stalybridge is a town near Manchester. The song is said to have been composed in the Newmarket Tavern. Jack Judge was challenged to write a song in one night. It is the chorus that is universally known, at least by the older generation in the UK:

> *It's a long way to Tipperary,*
> *It's a long way to go.*
> *It's a long way to Tipperary*
> *To the sweetest girl I know!*
> *Goodbye, Piccadilly,*
> *Farewell, Leicester Square!*
> *It's a long long way to Tipperary,*
> *But my heart's right there.*

The Tin Man of Nakasero

'**I have been foiled.**' In the early part of the last century most of the foil produced was made of tin. Cigarette packets were lined with it and sticks of chewing gum were wrapped in it. It was also used for wrapping leftover food. The problem was that it gave food a "tinny" taste like that of foods left for too long in a tin can. People still say 'tin foil' even though aluminium foil replaced it many years ago. Aluminium foil came into use in 1926. In this story the Tin Man is turned into tin foil. The expression 'tin-pot dictator' was at the back of my mind. This pejorative term was coined during the days of the British Empire and referred to the Victorian tin pot, a cheap container that was eventually replaced by the tin can in use today. A tin-pot dictator is defined by Wiktionary as "**an autocratic ruler with little political credibility, but with self-delusions of grandeur**". Bear in mind that the period these stories refer to encompasses the 1960s and the 1970s.

By the same author:

La poesía de Juan Larrea

Poemas a la Patagonia

Luton Poems

Nueve monedas para el barquero

El cuarto oscuro / The Dark Room

La casa de empeño / The Pawn Shop

A Night in Buganda

To Dylan

Dylan's Gower

El acantilado

www.ingramcontent.com/pod-product-compliance
Lightning Source LLC
Chambersburg PA
CBHW071303040426
42444CB00009B/1848